THE UNINTENDED CONSEQUENCES OF NOT LIVING FULLY

a memoir by
MARTHA J. MARTIN

TREATY OAK PUBLISHERS

PUBLISHER'S NOTE

This is a work of personal memoir and inspiration. All of the characters, business establish-ments, and events are based on the author's personal experiences. Individuals' names may have been changed to protect their privacy.

Printed and published in the United States of America

TREATY OAK PUBLISHERS

ISBN-10: 1-943658-25-0
ISBN-13: 978-1-943658-25-1

Revised Edition - Published September 5, 2019

DEDICATION

To my Water, Fire, and earth: I am your air
and while we are complete within
ourselves; we, too, are complete as one

To my parents

Deatra, you walked with me
throughout this journey without judgment,
you are the deepest definition of friend

CONTENTS

AUTHOR'S NOTE

Because some palpable expanse, invisible yet profuse—let's call it shame—had always kept me from exploring my deepest truths and validating them through words, I have only recently dreamed of becoming an author. And in my previous life, if I had ever possessed a notion that one day I'd write a memoir, this isn't the story I would have chosen for myself.

So why am I sharing it? Because the survival covenant I made with the Universe requires me to do so. And, after what I experienced between the front and back covers of this book, I no longer have a choice but to express myself fully and truthfully.

Truth is sacred.

• • •

The events that unfold in these pages are shared from solely my perspective. I also recognize that the thoughts *I think* others are having, are in fact one-hundred percent my own.

Depicted dialogue is from memory or journal entries, and most names, locations, and identifying characteristics have been changed to respect privacy.

PROLOGUE

I wasn't as much nervous about the appointment as I was stressed about missing work, finding the office building, and arriving late. As I entered the office area from the waiting room, I ran into a man who appeared to be a doctor… white medical coat. He turned and faced me as we made eye contact and said hello. His eyes then scanned the rest of my body.

I pretended not to notice.

My first encounter with the nurse was also dicey. I was given a diagram of a face and told to circle where I felt pain. I circled the area around my right temporomandibular joint, or "TMJ." She then asked me to step into another room for an x-ray of the joint.

I argued, "I'm only here for the bump in my cheek, not my jaw. My medical insurance doesn't cover TMJ issues."

She huffed, "I was told to take an x-ray."

After some back and forth protesting, I came to a level of agreement and allowed my face to be x-rayed. This particular type of x-ray machine takes panoramic shots that include both sides of the face. After the x-ray, I waited in the examining room for only a few minutes before the grumpy nurse came back and said she needed to take another x-ray. This time, I was instructed to open my mouth as wide as possible. I had no idea my wide-as-possible was half as wide as it should have been.

Back in the examining room, I learned that the wandering-eyed man I encountered earlier was the surgeon I was there to see, Dr. Christopher. His eyes were more professional this time.

While he pressed on my right cheek in the area around the bump, he asked, "How long have you been experiencing symptoms?"

"I noticed the bump about a year-and-a-half ago. It's since gotten larger and more tender. The jaw pain has been pretty constant for about five years or so."

Still pushing on my cheek, he said, "This mass is outside the area you circled on the diagram. I believe it's a tumor in your parotid gland. That's not something I can help you with, you need an ENT."

Dr. Christopher then informed me I had a second unrelated issue. He had ordered the second x-ray because he wanted a clearer shot of my right condyle. Pointing to an odd looking protrusion on the x-ray, he said, "I don't know what that is."

My right condyle appeared completely different than my left. In a matter-of-fact voice, he added, "You have two tumors on the right side of your face," qualifying that with, "That is what they are; that is what you call abnormal growths."

He asked the nurse to contact an otolaryngologist, or ear, nose, throat (ENT) doctor, with whom he maintained a professional relationship, to see if I could get an appointment as soon as possible. Pausing to contemplate, then referring to my right condyle, he said, "There's no one in Austin that can help you. It looks like bone... maybe calcification of the disc, but honestly, I've never seen anything like this."

It was a mystery. He paused in thought again. "There is only one person I would send you to, but you can't just call this guy up and make an appointment. He has to accept you."

"*Wonderful!*" In that moment of need, I learned that the only "guy" who could help me first had to judge whether my jaw was worthy of his time!

The appointment ended with reassuring words and an arm around my shoulder for an awkward half-hug as Dr. Christopher led me out to the desk of the woman trying to get me into see the ENT.

Success. "They can work you in tomorrow at 1:30. Is that okay?"

"Sure, I guess. Um… I'll be there."

Dr. Christopher chimed in, "This guy is at the Dallas-Fort Worth Metro Medical Center."

"I'm familiar with it."

"Great, but again, you can't just make an appointment. I have to write him a letter asking him to accept you."

Again, that word! *ACCEPT!*

"Dr. Marcus Kaye is his name, I'll write him this afternoon."

"Thanks."

"Let me know how it works out for you."

I agreed to follow-up with him, although I never did. Had this appointment not occurred at such a vulnerable time in my life, I may have handled it better. I also used to think… *if only* Dr. Christopher hadn't been creepy and had chosen his words more carefully… *if only* I had taken the time to digest and process his news in a healthy way… *if only* I had known how to scream.

We all have thousands of *if only* moments in our lives, and hundreds of perceived missteps that resulted in unintended consequences, or even altered our trajectories. Yet, because we can't know for certain where those old trajectories were going to deposit us, how can we define any moment, action, or inaction, as a mistake?

Maybe all our challenges are really just learning opportunities, nudges toward growth, gifts. And it is only after you learn, grow, and land somewhere completely unexpected that you recognize the past's trials as beautiful puzzle pieces, perfectly placed and laid out behind you.

Well, maybe not puzzle pieces; more like slats on a rollercoaster rail.

This rollercoaster ride began almost seven years before being told, "You have two tumors on the right side of your face."

On a Saturday evening in June 2004…

PART ONE

NOT PRACTICING SELF-CARE

The lack of a self-care practice
is a form of self-harm

Chapter 1
HIGHER LOVE

Steve Winwood's beats and wise words cut through torrents of rain and across the muddy field in which I was standing alone and crying. I wasn't physically alone, there were upwards of 90,000 other Bonnaroo revelers in that dark field outside of Manchester, Tennessee, including the elder of my two daughters, Lindsey. But, as Steve Winwood crooned on about higher love, I was lonely within my introspection, my honesty.

I want higher love. I wasn't sure what it felt like.

What I was certain of was that my life was about to change, and not in a way I wanted. I hoped to get through the weekend before the phone call came.

In the afternoon heat of day two, I stopped on my trek between performance tents to watch a heavy-set young man with an overstuffed backpack, shoulder-length dreads the same shade of brown as his shorts, and a faded black t-shirt from some past concert. He stood just outside the shade of a tent peering over the crowd. Every so often, he let go of his inhibitions and allowed the music to take over his body, twisting, gyrating, and stomping in sync with the music's energy. When inhibitions took over again, he'd stop dancing and stand still, separate from who he had just been. He remained motionless until he could no longer contain his dancing self and the music took over him once again. It was wonderful to witness.

I was jealous of his dancing self.

I did not see the weekend as the gift it was until it was over. The Bonnaroo Music Festival was a new experience for me, and I agonized over everything, real and perceived. Would I be able to get the rental car out of the mud? Could I even find the rental car? I worried about the abundance of mushrooms and the disturbing number of people who seemed to have consumed them. And although I would have greatly benefited from a single can of beer, fear had me sticking to water and Gatorade throughout the weekend.

It wasn't until Lindsey and I merged onto Interstate 24 to return to the Nashville airport—and ultimately to our home in Austin, Texas—that I was ready to embrace the circus of music, dancing, drugs, love, and peace we were leaving behind. In that moment, I longed for that circus to be my reality, and for the challenges I sensed down the road to be the fantasy.

• • •

Three days later, the phone call came. I was grateful it was from my mother, Abigail, because it could have come from most anyone—one of their neighbors or friends… adult protective services… the police.

At the time, I didn't appreciate how difficult it was for her to call me. She had never acknowledged her Alzheimer's, and both she and my dad had rebuffed past offers of assistance from my siblings and me. Rebuffed is putting it mildly when it came to my dad, Kelly, a former Marine. Not just *a Marine*, he was a World War II veteran – a Purple Heart and Bronze Star Drill Instructor who led troops into battles on Guam, Bougainville and Guadalcanal, and later Korea. He was a "you will eat what you are served and you will like it because it's better than eating bugs in the jungle" Marine.

Marines are self-reliant warriors, they're not supposed to be vulnerable. They're highly trained and skilled at not showing any weaknesses. Subsequently, my mother, my siblings, and I had successfully adapted into this mentality, building walls around us hiding any vulnerably or softness. This sadly had the consequence of suppressing expressions of love for one another. It was there, just not generously, or even openly, expressed. When is one more vulnerable than in a moment of expressing love?

Mom didn't directly ask for help. Her standard pleasantries were an attempt to mask her confusion and the anxiousness in her voice. She tried to explain that my dad's eye was getting worse and he had a doctor's appointment, but she didn't know when or where. She had an appointment card so I asked her to read it to me. The appointment was in two days.

"Mom, would you like me to come up and help get Dad into the doctor?"

With a single exhalation, the obstacles of self-preservation and pride she had been conditioned to place in front of her faded, at least temporarily.

"Oh, do you mind?"

I replied, "Of course not, I will be there tomorrow," at the same time thinking, *How am I going to explain this to my new boss?*

"Oh, thank you! Thank you so much!" Another exhalation. More relief.

• • •

I drove northward on a disheartening road into a city I'd escaped sixteen years earlier and toward the home I'd left before graduating high school. Located on the eastern edge of the West Texas dusty plains, Wichita Falls was a bio-dome of a city where conformity was celebrated and expectations and opportunities were scant for young women in the early 1980's who lacked structure and support.

Being financially responsible for myself while still in high school required working full-time and growing up too fast. Fear and other self-preservation skills kept me mostly safe during the eight months I was on my own. When Trey came along—with his handsome face and athletic build all cemented in a foundation of maturity, masculine kindness and honesty that was as foreign to me as a California sunset—he offered unrelenting love, security, stability and a zest for fun and adventure that I couldn't resist. His overtures were sincere but overwhelming, and I was eighteen and unsure. Before entering into a relationship with him, I consulted not with my family, but with my most reliable resources: music and my heart. Unsure how love was supposed to feel, Steve Winwood's *While You See a Chance* had reassured my eighteen-year-old heart and convinced it to venture on Trey. We married six months later.

This is the memory that had besieged me at Bonnaroo while standing in the rain. *How could I have made such a huge life decision based on a song?* The recollection had prompted doubts and tears as fresh lyrics sparked a yearning for something more for the future, *a higher love.*

For years I had intended to address my unhappiness in the marriage, to resolve all those little resentments that had stacked up inside me over the decades, *once I cross this next hurdle.* But with each successful leap, I'd always find another one of life's hurdles awaiting.

Two weeks before Lindsey and I attended Bonnaroo, my youngest daughter, Meredith, graduated from high school. Getting her out of high school had just been my latest excuse; now I was driving into the unknown challenges of caring for parents who were no longer capable of caring for themselves.

Chapter 2
THE WARRIOR

The states of my dad's health and living condition were worse than I anticipated based on my mother's descriptions. I should have expected that. He had been to a physician at some point because he had a couple of bottles of medication and some eye drops sitting on his nightstand. Mom had been regularly refilling a glass of water, but not cleaning it. It was lined with a thick gel-like film that explained his complaint of diarrhea.

He had been getting out of bed only to go to the bathroom and was dependent on Mom to bring him food, which I don't think was happening often enough based on his level of weakness. This had been the state of his existence for several weeks, and, with no vision in one eye and no concept of time, he seemed perfectly content.

The inevitable occurred upon our arrival at the ophthalmologist's office. Our parent-child roles officially flipped. I was now in charge and they accepted it; they were relieved. The ophthalmologist confirmed my dad had suffered a stroke within his left eye and its vision could not be restored. He needed surgery to cauterize the bleeding which was beyond what the ophthalmologist could perform. In discussing this with the doctor, who had already asked a nurse to contact a Dallas surgeon, I requested a referral to an Austin-based one instead. No way could my parents remain in Wichita Falls alone. Having my dad's eye surgery performed in Austin would allow him to recover safely in my home. I also thought it would ease their transition from living independently.

My parents' transition into assisted living was tumultuous at best. The greatest challenge over the remaining summer of 2004 was attempting, and failing miserably, to balance both of my parents' needs and happiness while they suffered from different types of dementia at varying levels of progression. My dad's needs were obviously imminent. The Marine was now vulnerable and at times heartbreakingly fragile.

All he really needed—where he found peace—was in a quiet comfortable space where he felt secure, cared for, and knew his wife of 52 years was relatively attentive. Disruptions in his peace or sense of security set off his angry warrior, his highly developed survival instincts that had served him well in the South Pacific. He could be quite frightening during those times, but not inconsolable.

Although he'd been prescribed a topical sedative, whenever his confusion, insecurity, and questions swelled, I was able to calm him with gentle words, a loving touch, and by playing Norah Jones' CD, *Come Away with Me.* His reaction was always the same. About twenty seconds into *Don't Know Why,* he'd notice the melody and then the voice. After about a minute he would say, "Eeewee, that's beautiful!"

Listening. Calming. Serenity by track two. He heard that CD a hundred times that summer, but every time was a new and wondrous experience for him.

I credit my dad for my love of music. One thing we had in common, but just one of most everything we never discussed. Without the luxury of a television for many years of my childhood, music was the favored substitute. I have colorful memories of my dad flashing new albums he'd just bought. The woman stretched out in a chair with wild clothes and pink feathers in her hair was Janice Joplin; then there was the playful animation of the Beatles' Yellow Submarine. I danced alone around our small living room with the same carefree spirit of the music that compelled me, bounding off the couch and between chairs, wailing along with the lyrics.

The soundtrack of my childhood consists of artists and songs all introduced to me by my dad: Bob Dylan; Peter, Paul and Mary; Joan Baez; Simon and Garfunkel; Johnny Cash; Woody Guthrie; and more. Artists and songs that reflected his true nature and contrasted with the Marine he was supposed to be.

Once in my care, I struggled to make the rest of his days as blissful as the peace he found in Norah Jones' voice. That was an impossible task. He was too sick, too confused, and I couldn't constantly be at his side to calm him. With one daughter in college and another just entering, I had to work.

Through a series of peace-disrupting doctor appointments, MRI's, and a whole battery of other tests, Dad was diagnosed with vascular dementia resulting from a series of small strokes related to previously undiagnosed high blood pressure. Dad's memory issues appeared only two years earlier and had progressed beyond the level of Mom's. For the past decade, she would telephone and carry on the same happy conversation from days before. With Dad, he no longer remembered how or whom to call.

The greatest disturber of my dad's peace was the constant reoccurrence of urinary tract infections. The perfect storm conditions of infection and dementia set off rages, sometimes violent, that were fed by feverous hallucinations. Once antibiotics kicked in, he retreated to the sweet, gentle, and fragile man who could be calmed.

After my sister, Susan, arrived from Washington, D.C., to tour facilities with Mom, my parents quickly settled into a small assisted living apartment near my home in early July. The nursing care and reviews were good and I lived nearby, allowing for daily visits and close monitoring of their care. It was cozy, and Dad settled in beautifully. He had his comforts of home with his own furniture, select books and artwork, but it was my mom's presence that reassured him. Most essential to my mother was Northside Manor's décor – she loved the floral prints of forest green, pink, gold, and burgundy. "It feels like home."

Of course, weighing Mom's opinions against exactly how much she understood was impossible, but Northside Manor seemed perfect. Dad's urinary tract infections were monitored and treated, and the small setting with simple routines suited him well. His senses of contentment and safety returned, and I was able to resume a regular work routine.

The biggest mistake made that summer was focusing too much on my dad's needs while not recognizing my mom's loss of her sense of community, friends, independence, and need for social engagement. After three weeks, the coziness and simplicity that had helped to calm Dad became isolating and tedious for my mother. Despite being surrounded by her favored hues, Mom was unhappy and began verbally acting out toward Dad.

Less than a month after moving into assisted living, my fun-loving, optimistic, happy, social butterfly of a mother stuffed an entire roll of bathroom tissue into their toilet and flooded the apartment. I received the call at work and was told to move them out immediately.

Although there had been no evidence of Mom physically harming Dad, her actions prompted Northside Manor to contact adult protective services. I was both mortified and exasperated. All decisions and actions had been made solely in the interests of health and safety. Mom could get upset, but I'd never seen her angry, and she definitely had never been violent.

We found the second facility with the assistance of a case manager. Hilltop Manor was much larger with multiple floors and tastefully decorated to my mother's standards. The demographics were heavily weighted on the female side and residents moved freely and readily throughout the many hallways, activity rooms, and indoor and outdoor gathering spaces.

At the advice of the case manager, they had separate rooms: a standard room for Dad on the second floor near the dining room; and for Mom, an efficiency studio two floors above. With some sense of independence and loads of potential new friends, she required no adjusting whatsoever. She had, this time, actually found her home. She was happy, which helped her receive a passing grade by adult protective services.

The larger, bustling environment and confusion with having my mom living two floors up increased Dad's anxiety. Susan flew to Austin again and spent the first several days of Dad's transition sleeping in a recliner next to his bed. Afterwards, we arranged for a health care worker to sit with him during the day, and I stopped by in the evenings after work to join them for dinner.

Through daily visits and leaving bright sticky notes all over Dad's apartment reminding him where he was, where he could find Mom, and of other matters that could potentially cause him concern, Dad regained a sense of security by early September. The health care worker was released, and we all settled into a new normal – a new normal that lasted about ten days.

With the focus on his transition, and less than stringent medical monitoring, a full-blown urinary tract infection developed and caused Dad to faint while eating breakfast. EMS was called and paramedics hovered over him, checking his vital signs as he regained consciousness. He was conscious, but not lucid, and his angry warrior felt threatened and fought off the paramedics.

When I arrived at the emergency room, he was lucid and calm. The intravenously fed antibiotics had an immediate effect so I could only imagine what had transpired before my arrival. I kept up a positive persona for his sake, but was crying on the inside at the sight of this fragile man with enough fight in him to merit having his ankles and wrists strapped to the hospital bed.

Following the fainting episode, one of Hilltop Manor's nurses was adamant that my dad should not be allowed to return. I had been responsible for my parent's care for three months, and they were about to be kicked out of a second assisted living facility.

Thankfully, Hilltop Manor's head nurse was more sympathetic to my dad's condition. She would allow him to return if he passed a psychological evaluation. A geriatric psychologist conducted the evaluation the next morning. Dad easily passed and the psychologist stated he could return to an assisted living setting.

When I relayed the report to the head nurse, she backed out of our initial agreement. She betrayed me, and more importantly, she betrayed my dad. I had no time to think about that or argue with her. The hospital was releasing him within the hour and I was offered a non-negotiable compromise. The only way Dad could return—where his wife was settled and happy and where we had worked so diligently to get him settled—was to have him committed to a psychiatric ward for further testing and monitoring to assure he was not a harm to others.

A crushing blow after witnessing everything he had just suffered. The crying on my inside turned to screaming. He had done nothing wrong consciously. He was not the bad person they thought he was. If he had been properly monitored for infection, he wouldn't have passed out and ended up in the hospital, and I wouldn't be faced with having to commit him! I felt powerless against the situation and the legal and social structures.

I did not try to explain the situation to him. Even if he understood its gravity, he would not remember it. And, what if he had not agreed? Neither of us could have endured the hearings and timely process associated with involuntary commitments. So, without his knowledge or consent, I signed his name to the voluntary commitment form.

Austin's senior adult psychiatric facility was located in the same building as the hospital from which he was about to be released. After signing the commitment and hospital release forms, I helped him into a wheelchair and escorted him up the elevators to the psych ward. He was pleasant, in agreement with, and understanding of the fact he was, "going to stay in another area of the hospital to help get you back to where Mom is."

It wasn't a complete lie. I handed the paperwork to the nurse and security guard supervising the entrance and we were buzzed into the ward. As I rolled Dad's wheelchair over the threshold, the part of me that had been screaming surrendered, and it felt as if something inside me died.

Susan already had plans to return to Austin the coming weekend to attend the Austin City Limit's Musical Festival, "ACL." She flew in a few days early and took over communicating with psychiatrists, nurses, and Hilltop Manor's administrators while I tried to maintain a presence at work.

Dad was a trooper. He seemed to realize where he was by day two, and perhaps that frightened him because he was on his best behavior. He was released after a week and allowed to return to Hilltop Manor where he settled back into a routine.

I continued through the next five months trying my best to balance work, run a household, be a mother to daughters in colleges 2,000 miles away, and assure through almost daily visits that my parents were stable, and their physical and emotional needs were met. I did this with little sleep and a heavy and constant sense that I was failing them all.

By late January 2005, Dad stopped getting up for breakfast. He caused small conflicts when some of the less-than-caring care associates attempted to bring him breakfast. Despite the level of his dementia, he maintained a keen sense of who was afraid of him, who did not like him and who did, and he reacted accordingly. Soon it got to the point that it was easier for me to get him breakfast on my way to work. He was sweet in the mornings, always glad to see me and appreciative for his breakfast.

One morning in early February, I was rushed more than usual because it was "board meeting day" at work, and my boss seemed to hold me responsible if some aspect of the meeting did not go smoothly. I didn't let that keep me from assuring Dad had a good breakfast. In fact, I had a very strong sense I needed to make sure he had a warm, hearty breakfast. Because I arrived earlier than usual, the only breakfast options available at Hilltop Manor were yogurt and muffins. I followed my inner voice and raced to a nearby grocery store to get him a hot breakfast from the store's deli. I returned with scrambled eggs, sausage patties, and a handful of large, fresh, gorgeous strawberries.

When I entered his room, I found him as I had left him the evening before. He had slept in his recliner, wearing his khaki pants and a white undershirt stained with morsels from previous meals. He thanked me with a refreshing happiness and carried on about how good breakfast was with each bite.

"Eeewee! This is the best sausage I've ever eaten."

"Eeewee! These are the best strawberries!"

He was in heaven with each bite, taking an entire strawberry into his mouth and then spitting out the hull. After he'd eaten, I helped him into a clean shirt, covered his legs with a blanket, and kissed him on the cheek. As I turned to leave, I breached the protocol in which I had been raised. "I love you, Daddy."

He responded faintly, his words were strained but delivered with sincere tenderness, "Love you, too."

And I shut the door behind me.

I arrived at work 30 minutes before the board meeting was to begin – very late by my standards and by my boss' obvious expectations. It was unusual for me not to care about that, but I did not.

An hour and half into the meeting, a co-worker retrieved me to take a phone call. My dad had been found lying on the floor of his room with no pulse. Paramedics had tried to revive him to no avail. My first thought as I hung up the phone was that I had failed him. Everything I had done was not enough to keep him from dying. A ridiculous thought, but that is how one thinks while living under the delusion that they are in control.

Chapter 3
ABIGAIL'S TRUE SELF

Susan would later comment that she had "abandoned" me and Mom when she left for a sailing trip around the world. But the only time I felt a hint of abandonment was the evening of my father's funeral, Valentine's Day 2005. Each sibling and grandchild attended his burial service at Dallas' National Cemetery following a weekend family gathering in Austin and a memorial service in Wichita Falls. With return flights booked for Monday evening, we all caravanned back to Austin following Dad's burial.

It was a whirlwind afternoon and evening between getting Mom settled back into her apartment and getting family to the airport, including my own daughters. The fact that it was Valentine's Day and my mother had just buried her husband of 52 years did not set in until the chaos of the day dissipated. It was dark by the time Trey and I returned to her apartment with a small floral arrangement. She appreciated it and was happy when I said goodnight and left.

Having not eaten, but lacking a full appetite, Trey and I headed to a nearby restaurant for dessert. As I sat in an iron patio chair, eating chocolate decadence cake under the soft gleam of red and white twinkle lights, I imagined my mother admiring the flowers and feeling happy in her apartment overlooking the Texas Hill Country. *What's missing?*

My siblings had all vanished, heading back to the same lives they lived before while my life would remain not completely my own. The vastness of Mom's needs, her care and happiness, settled en masse onto my shoulders – an unpredictable collection of unknowns that I would be responsible for carrying. The bitter and resentful thoughts, directed at both her and my siblings, hovered just outside of me, floating nearby within grasp, as if I had a choice with what to do with them. I thought about how those emotions could negatively affect me, my happiness and ability to confront the oncoming challenges. In that moment, I resolved to no longer embrace resentment and bitterness, at least not toward my siblings.

I was also aware that my parenting standards had been powered by a steadfast determination to be a better mother than Abigail, so it was with slight resentment that I thought, *You're my mother, I love you. I will take care of you… I will take great care of you.*

With time, Trey and I settled into another new normal, and life was mostly manageable over the course of the next five years. My schedule was divided among meeting the demands of work, maintaining a household, overseeing Mom's care, and the occasional personal and physical challenges of long-distance motherhood. The average week consisted of working 40 to 50 hours, visiting my mother after work, and getting her out on weekends to visit the grocery store, catch a movie, eat Mexican food, drive through the Hill Country, or some combination thereof. The remaining weekend I spent catching up on mail, bills, and chores, while trying to squeeze in some personal time with Trey for a hike or dinner and a movie. Yes, our relationship was the last priority.

Mom's Alzheimer's disease was slow progressing, and I became well attuned to her state of being and needs, like a mother is with her child. I noticed every slight decrease in her cognition, of which there were numerous, and tried to make each downward step as stress-free on her as possible. A loving presence and patience proved to be most effective until a medication tweak kicked in.

I was aware that each tweak was a temporary fix and that she would continue on a path into nothingness. But I never took the time between fixes to grieve the little bit of her I had just lost. I just kept showing up the next day with a smile. That is what *she* needed, and I had learned early on that it was best to enter her world.

It certainly was necessary in helping her maintain her denial – Mom chose to deal with her Alzheimer's diagnosis by not dealing with it. My parents were of the silent generation; unpleasant or uncomfortable matters were either downplayed or outright ignored and denied.

I understood and even related to Abigail's level of pride. I was happy to go into her world to help her maintain her self-preservation and subsequently, her senses of joy and happiness, which at times was fun.

One entertaining phone call came after she began having trouble keeping up with the keys to her room because she kept hiding them and then forgetting where. After again "losing" the keys for a few days, she called and proudly proclaimed she discovered what had happened to them.

"What happened, Mom? Where were they?"

"Hillary Clinton had them!"

"Oh, well… I'm so glad she gave them back to you!"

• • •

By the end of September 2009, Mom's disease had progressed to the point that Hilltop Manor's administrator felt it was no longer safe for her to remain in the larger assisted living environment. I was told that she would be transitioned into the secured living area, the "memory unit." I can only guess the administrator used the word "transition" to appease and avoid challenging what she probably recognized in me as some level of denial. I often had unrealistic understandings of Mom's mental and physical capacities, or lack thereof. The micro-perspective I maintained on the state of her well-being protected me from seeing the bigger picture. My own senses of denial and defense I had so aptly learned from her.

ACL weekend approached again. I always looked forward to the Austin City Limits Music Festival as a fun-filled distraction, a respite weekend. *Music is my medicine!* However, more times than not, some parent-related crisis or predicament took precedence. In 2004, it was my dad's transition from the psychiatric ward back into assisted living. In 2009, it was moving and settling my mom into a new, small, locked, less than private, and based on the energy levels of the other residents, less than cheerful home.

She was not happy. It was a setback. The stress of the move and adjustment caused her to lose a little bit more of herself. To have to weigh the concern for a loved one's safety against the physical and mental cost of the actions taken to address that concern is a cruel and impossible task. A cost covered by another eventual effective tweak in medication.

I defined my mother's decline in cognition by how old she seemed to be based on her awareness, abilities, vocabulary, innocence, and need for sleep. She was eight when she was made to move into the memory unit, but the transition turned her to age seven by the year's end.

Her regression to six by the spring of 2010 was accompanied by a mix of anxiety and agitation that reduced her to age five by autumn of the same year. The anxiety and agitation occurred primarily in the evenings, "sundowner's syndrome." Although this stage of her disease was challenging, she and I endured it together. On evenings when she was particularly distressed, I lay with her until she fell asleep and on occasion, I spent the night with her.

The anxiety and agitation subsided in early 2011. The price of her finding peace at last was that she had lost most of herself. As the pieces of Abigail sadly faded away, I welcomed and needed the beautiful advantage: in her childlike state, she had no judgments or self-preservation skills; just the pure, innocent love of her true self.

I fondly referred to this time as "Martha's Revenge." That's "revenge" in a subtle, loving sense. You see Abigail had not been doting, affectionate, or attentive. Had she been born later and come of age in the 1960's after "the pill" and during the women's liberation movement, I think she may have opted to not have children, at least not four of them. Born only eight years after women in the U.S. gained the right to vote, she was a child of the Great Depression. The social schemes of her time offered young women a future of marriage and motherhood. The marriage aspect seemed to have suited her well and I know she loved all her children, but she never seemed to embrace motherhood.

Being ever so human, Abigail preferred that which augmented her self-image and self-esteem. As the youngest child I never sensed that I fulfilled that need. I had not been special. Mom appeared to favor her baubles, her friends and her job. Even when I was too young to possess the capacity to label or protest her neglectful tendencies, I understood that she did not want to be bothered.

When I was a young teen she was more direct in affirming what I already perceived, telling me on multiple occasions, "I'm tired of being a mother." At age 19, after I'd given birth to her first grandchild, she acknowledged to my sister that I was raised through "benevolent neglect." I never asked my parents what exactly that meant. *So you neglected me, but that was okay because you loved me?*

By the time Abigail had regressed to age four in January 2011, and as the weight of my schedule, responsibilities, and life wore on me, our roles re-reverted. I was again the daughter who longed for a feeling of connectedness to her. This time, though, she would let me hug her, hold her hand, brush her thick curly hair, and paint her fingernails. In her presence, defenses, pretenses and perceptions were no longer necessary, and her world provided an escape from mine.

Just as I was not aware of, or had simply not allowed, grieving that should have taken place over each progressing stage of my mother's disease, I also was not conscious of how much I had come to rely on her as a source of love and affection.

Chapter 4
COMFORTABLE RUTS

Humans are complex beings with behaviors driven by countless combinations of infinite variables. When two humans come together in a covenant of partnership or marriage the outcome always equals complexity squared.

• • •

Having two children within the first three years of our marriage, Trey's and my relationship evolved and revolved around our daughters. They were the number one priority, and Trey and I had both sacrificed to grow and maintain a strong, healthy, loving, cohesive family. We loved each other, and we loved being a family.

As young parents we had established goals of creating great childhood memories for our daughters, and providing them the best opportunities and growth experiences possible. And we had done a great job.

Trey was an amazing father, he was the fun one… the playmate who taught his girls how to fish, play cards and sports. He was the planner of regular fun-filled vacations, and I was the serious mediator of it all, assuring there was a proper balance between the fun and responsibilities.

But it wasn't all rosy. We are humans; we came with thorns.

Trey had abandonment issues that sometimes caused him to be overbearing and jealous. I was the perfectionist striving to recreate the idyllic images in my head that dictated what we all should look like and what we should be doing. This often clashed with Trey's deep-seated needs to control and receive only positive affirmations. Our polar-opposite outlooks were also sources of quarrels. I was the blind optimist, and Trey was the ever-questioning, "there's got to be a catch!" pessimist. Or as he would state, "I'm a realist," but I defined him as, "the popper of balloons."

With many of our squabbles, I conceded defeat rather than push subjects to the point of full-blown arguments… Trey's temper was his most effective defense mechanism, and I was an abiding peacekeeper. That's how most of those old resentments came to be smoldering inside of me, and why they remained unresolved. My other grudges, I must admit, were the result of Trey's failure to fulfill my unrealistic perceptions of the perfect husband.

As our daughters neared college age, Trey's and my time outside of work continued to be filled and fulfilled by being a family. We relished in our daughters' accomplishments, cheered for them in extracurricular sports, and supported them through the excitement and stress of college visits and applications. Before Meredith's high school graduation, I felt my own personal precipice approaching. I didn't know what it would look like once I reached the cliff's edge, but was ready for a change.

I could no longer tolerate the unhealthy aspects of our marriage, and I wanted a different life. But because of his defenses and staunch aversion to change, I wasn't sure that life would include Trey.

That would have been an appropriate time for Trey and me to have an actual conversation about our relationship and what we wanted the other side of that cliff to look like. We didn't have that conversation. Instead, the responsibilities of caring for my parents more than occupied the time I had previously focused on our daughters, and Trey's career consumed his focus.

These shifts in priorities allowed for the natural development of a convenient routine of existing without dealing with our relationship issues. Our conversations never crept below the surface and were limited to topics related to our daughters, our dog, home and auto maintenance, the latest movie, the weather, what to watch on television, and where or what to eat.

The fact that I am a morning person and Trey a night person was helpful while raising our daughters. Well after I left for work he'd stick around and see the girls off to school. I'd return home in the late afternoon for soccer practice, homework, and to throw dinner together.

Once both girls were in college, we continued with our natural sleep routines. During many work weeks, we did not see or speak to each other face to face. I was up and off to work before either the sun or Trey rose, and would be asleep before he came home.

Summer "vacation" time was spent moving one or both of our daughters to/from the northeastern U.S. where they attended school. This is how our relationship existed as the weeks, seasons and years passed. We walked in circles, around and around, dredging a path comprised of regular routines and unspoken words. I desired change, but life had taken over and I allowed my unhappiness, my truth, to lie dormant while waiting for a break from the non-stop challenges.

I found balance for my discontentment at home with success at work. By late 2008, my career was at last pointing in a desirable direction. I had been able to break from the executive assistant label through hard work, long hours, dedication, and a prideful tenacity to prove my abilities. With my new job as a program and communications specialist, an identity I never wanted had been lifted, and in my mind, I was professionally liberated and somewhat validated.

I had originally accepted the administrative tract when I was thrust into adulthood with plenty of insecurities, and not enough wherewithal to conceive the notion of options. Although I had always wanted more for myself, I heeded the external messages that I consciously and subconsciously received. Those messages had me living down to other people's expectations, staying within the limiting perimeters of my perceptions of other people's perceptions, and accepting the patriarchal world I observed growing up in Wichita Falls as the youngest child of a Marine. I carried all this into adulthood and the governmental environment of my employment.

Perhaps my career path would have been different if I had a mentor through high school, or at least someone who expressed belief in me, or saw me as special or possessing potential. Perhaps it would have been different if I had believed any of this about myself. I did to an extent, just not enough to challenge my perceptions of the status quo.

That is, until I mustered up the courage to ask for a job change that should have been granted years before... *all I had to do was use my voice to speak up for myself and ask.*

This taste of liberation of my true self, at least the working part of myself, played a large role in the next significant act of my story.

About six months before Mom's move into the memory unit, I was working late in my new office cubical that sat along a fourth floor wall of floor-to-ceiling windows. Sitting at my computer was like balancing on a glorious ledge overlooking East Austin and a corner of the University of Texas campus. I didn't mind working late, as I could see the log jam of cars idling on the elevated section of Interstate 35. I was treated to the reflection of the sunset on the eastern clouds and UT's football stadium. I'd watch darkness take over the city, illuminating office lights and prompting car headlights. I loved my cubicle, and I loved my new job.

As I basked in that moment, a glimpse of the gold band on my left ring finger brought my attention to another reality. Another part of myself was not so happy. This part had yet to muster courage, or find a voice.

Trey's and my already well-worn comfortable rut grew deeper that evening as I removed the ring from my finger and placed it in my desk drawer organizer among the pens, pencils, and paperclips. As I closed the drawer, I wondered whether Trey would notice. A part of me hoped he would. Maybe the act of removing the band, in part, was my attempt to start the hard conversations that needed to take place. If he did ever notice, he never said anything. That's how life works in a comfortable rut.

· · ·

Our health was another neglected aspect of our lives. We had allowed our jobs, my mother's needs, and everything else on our plates to take precedence. Together, the states of our relationship and health resulted in Trey withdrawing physically from me just as I had withdrawn from him emotionally… more bluntly, we stopped having sex.

Trey's eating habits and lack of exercise positioned him to adhere to my reality without having to acknowledge it. As for me, I just felt bad. My mind and body were exhausted, I had ignored pain in my right jaw for years, and began experiencing intermittent burning sensations along the left side of my sternum in early 2010.

Although I had started taking yoga classes and enjoyed their positive effects on my strength, posture, and stress levels, I let work and other priorities keep me from attending classes for months at a time. It seemed like I was always having to start over on building strength and finding calm.

During an extended break from yoga, the burning in my chest elevated and forced me to have it checked out. In early March 2010, my elder brother, Peter, came from Nevada for a visit. He arrived on Friday evening and we caught up over a dinner of Mexican food. I made it through dinner, but could not force myself to sleep through the slicing pain radiating through my back. I rose with the sun, dressed, and quietly slipped out the door and into my car while my brother and family slept. I called the after-hours clinic on the drive, hopeful they would have an opening or be able to work me in. I first assured the duty nurse that the burning pain was not my heart, but as soon as she connected the words "chest" and "pain," she stopped listening and told me to head immediately to the Austin Heart Hospital.

I was more frustrated by the fact that she didn't believe me. "But it's not my heart! And it's not heartburn. The burning is between my esophagus and chest cavity!"

By the time I hung up the phone, I was in tears. The stress of the conversation caused the burning rod sensation to elevate and cut more through the center of my chest and out between my spine and left shoulder blade. I took a deep breath and forced calm, then headed to the heart hospital. I did not call Trey or either daughter to let them know.

As I stood at the emergency room admitting window and relayed what was going on, I was a cool cucumber. All evidence of tears was gone. An attendant escorted me into an examining room as I again explained the pain I experienced. "It's not my heart, it's to the right of my heart and feels like really bad heartburn, but heartburn that's outside of my esophagus."

Probably not a sensible medical statement, but I described it exactly as it felt. It was not my heart, as I had a keen awareness of my body. My heart was fine. I could feel it; nothing was going on there. In fact, I was calmer than all those attending to me, yet I was prescribed anxiety medication after all the diagnostics, tests, and x-rays confirmed exactly what I had been stating. Nothing was wrong with my heart.

I picked up the anxiety prescription on my way home. *Who was I to question a physician?*

While at work the prior day, I noticed a raw patch of skin between my shoulder blade and left armpit and assumed my shirt was too tight and had chafed the skin. I had talked myself out of mentioning it while in the ER. The physician and nurses already believed I was anxious, so I wasn't about to point out my raw patch of back fat that I'd already concluded was caused by a tight shirt. If I had, they might have gotten the diagnosis correct. Within days, the raw patch increased in size and more red whelps spread out across my left breast. Shingles.

Ten days later, a close family member died. Steve's death was not unexpected. I knew what our loved ones in Houston were going through. I could feel the weight of their distress. Unlike the bitterness and resentment I felt floating outside of me following my dad's funeral, I could not choose to sweep these emotions away. They were the result of a hard reality I could not change. So, these emotions remained near me, not properly acknowledged or acted upon throughout Steve's final days; and they had eaten away at my immune system.

In the weeks following Steve's funeral, the shingle's rash showed signs of healing. Yet, I continued to feel terribly weak and achy. I hadn't taken time off work or from my hectic schedule, and the effects of shingles lingered on, as did the mental and physical exhaustion leading up to them.

One April morning while at work, I stepped into my office's kitchenette and found that someone had left some pastries on the counter to share. I normally would have helped myself to one, but this morning, I had no appetite for them. I had felt so bad for so long that the sight of them disgusted me. I knew eating one would only make me feel worse, so I vowed to no longer eat anything except food that made me feel better. Food that provided energy rather than zapping it. The notion that I could make myself feel better was empowering.

Steve's death and the current stage of my mother's disease were motivators as well, but foremost, I was tired of being tired and feeling terrible. As I returned to my office and sat down, I promised myself I would also stop letting work take priority over my yoga practice.

These two simple decisions, made just minutes apart, had immediate transformative effects on my body, overall health, state of mind, and energy level. I had been slow to learn the lesson, but I finally got it. *I need to take care of my body.*

• • •

Energy.

I was four when I first acknowledged the precious power of energy. The memory of being bed ridden with an early summer bout of pneumonia is vague; however, I recall vivid details of an evening later that summer. I had recovered enough to play with my siblings in our front yard where my parents sat in lawn chairs and talked. Darkness had taken over and I was working on emptying a Pez dispenser while galloping about at each sight of a flickering firefly. As I downed each candy capsule, I told my siblings they were energy pills, except "energy" would come out "injury," which would make them laugh.

I didn't understand why they laughed at me, and was frustrated because my energy pills were very important. The pneumonia had traumatized me a bit because I not only had a strange need to take energy pills, I also contrived imaginary doctors – Dr. Kay and Dr. Dee. I was happy to have Drs. Kay and Dee caring for me as they made me feel special and provided me with senses of comfort and security.

Unlike my childhood magical "energy" pills, yoga and eating well worked to help me climb out of one of my comfortable ruts, but I was alone in that endeavor. My energy, positive outlook, self-awareness, and overall awareness all increased, as did my confidence while thriving under the challenges of my new job.

Each time Trey rebuffed my pleas to take better care of himself, the space between us—that silent sphere of discontent—widened. He dug deeper into his comfortable rut of routines, and I further buried my resentments as other aspects of life expanded, and as life's hurdles continued to pop up.

That summer had Lindsey moving into her own home and Meredith returning home to save money. We also began renovations on our house. It was not my choice to renovate; that was Trey's compromise. I wanted to move out of the Austin suburbs and near downtown and work. For twenty-one years, I had commuted and the traffic got worse each year. The commute contributed to my exhaustion and resentment toward Trey. I first expressed my desire to leave the suburbs after Meredith's high school graduation. So at this point, I had harbored that grudge for six years.

Mia, our beautiful white German shepherd, had seizures soon after the renovation started. Mia was the glue in our family as we navigated through the many challenges that arose soon after we adopted her. Her presence provided unlimited sources of joy, play, love, and companionship. It was heart wrenching to watch Mia suffer through the seizures. The vet was pretty certain the seizures and the onset of breathing difficulties were the result of a tumor on her pituitary gland, common in dogs. The anti-seizure medication worked at first, but the seizures returned and the dosage was increased. Sometimes the adjustment worked for a couple of months, sometimes it lasted a couple of weeks.

Trey, Meredith, and I kept watch over Mia when we were home, which was sufficient for about five months and as the seizures appeared to be occurring only in the evenings. Over the same timeframe, Mom was nearing the end stage of Alzheimer's. So, both Mom and Mia experienced disruptive evenings and required frequent medication adjustments. Leaving work each evening became overwhelming as I was forced to somehow balance my loyalties and time between the two. My mother was in a safe environment and receiving high quality care, but was declining. Monitoring her welfare had become engrained into my after-work routine. For the preceding six-and-a-half years, I'd leave work, walk to the parking garage across the street from my office, ascend the stairwell to the floor where I parked my maroon Mazda Tribute, sit behind its wheel, and let my autopilot steer me to Hilltop Manor.

Mia stayed inside after the seizures began. We made sure an area was covered with pee pads, and, like when our daughters were young, Trey handled the morning shift. He fed, walked, and medicated Mia before leaving for work. I arrived home in the early evening to let her out, give her more medication, and clean up the pee pad messes. By the end of the year, Mia experienced seizures during the day while we were at work. She also lost either the ability or will to make it to the pee pads, so we closed off the carpeted rooms, but the main living areas all had to be covered. We lived with wall-to-wall pee pads, and what was already a difficult routine turned intolerable and ridiculous to maintain. I believed the only logical solution was to put Mia down. Guilt always followed this thought, she still seemed to maintain a joy for life and my family was not ready to let her go.

I maintained the unbearable routine and absorbed the daily internal conflict of having to choose between my mother and my dog. Now when I climbed into my Tribute after work, I wanted to steer it into a deep, isolated, quiet, black hole and disappear.

I hated my life at home. It was too hard, too much; the ridiculously long commute; my mom's ongoing deterioration; the not knowing what I would face with her from one day to the next; and not knowing what I would face at home with Mia every evening. Oh, there would be dog mess to pick up. So, that was a sure thing.

I expressed my feelings of exhaustion and frustration to Trey, but just those related to Mia. Nothing changed, and I soon came to believe that Trey held my well-being second to Mia's. Not recognizing my own passivity, I'd also long concluded that my wants and needs came after Trey's own.

Opting to carry on with my daily impossible choices, I harbored even more disdain for him. Our quiet chasm widened while I maintained commitments to a regular yoga practice and healthy eating. My waist had reformed, I gained muscles for the first time since childhood and good posture for the first time ever.

Outside of my home, I was happy and thriving. I recognized this, but justified that perhaps that is what a "balanced life" is supposed to look like.

Chapter 5
HE HAS TO ACCEPT YOU

The contrasts between my external and internal voices seemed to manifest within my body. My right side felt alien, completely different from my left. The pain in the area of my right jaw had worsened and, although I mentioned it during well visits, my primary care physician never expressed concern and thought it was probably due to stress. *Why would I question that?*

She told me to let my dentist know, and when I consulted with a dentist at regular check-ups, he said it was a medical issue and to consult my doctor. This back-and-forth carried on for several years.

In early 2010, I made a weak attempt to obtain a medical referral to an oral surgeon; however, I hung up on my health insurance carrier after being transferred once and holding for 10 minutes. Had I called on behalf of my mother or one of my daughters, I would have never conceded so easily.

During a follow-up appointment with my family doctor, I also was not persistent when trying to point out a bump that had developed in my right cheek. My doctor didn't feel the bump, nor was she concerned with the pain and muscle atrophy in my right shoulder. In fact, when I looked at her straight away and told her, "It feels like something's wrong with the right side of my body," she stared back at me blankly as if I were crazy. This was shortly after my experience at the heart hospital ER, where they, too, thought I was crazy.

By the end of 2010, and after a difficult year with my mother as she transgressed through another Alzheimer's stage, the tension in my right jaw radiated up into my temple, down my neck, and into my shoulder, breast, and arm. From time to time, I also experienced pain in my hip joint and down into my leg, but continued to accept my physician's opinion that it was the result of something I had been doing. I tried to be conscious of how I sat at my desk and computer; how I held my shoulders when I drove, and I'd made progress. Before making yoga a regular practice, I couldn't lift my right arm above my shoulder. Yoga expanded its mobility by about 45 degrees, and I looked like I was signaling an airplane to veer right when I held my arms above my head to stretch. That was progress.

When it came time for the next six-month dental cleaning, I decided to see the dentist Trey had been using. With no trouble, she found the bump in my cheek and recommended I see an oral surgeon. I waited two months, until I had a day off work, to attempt the referral process again. On President's Day, after seven phone calls and four hours of frustration, tears, and pleading, I secured the referral and scheduled an appointment with an oral surgeon.

• • •

The personal challenges of being solely responsible for the care of a loved one include not just the time and physical aspects. No, what truly takes a toll are the mental and spiritual challenges – what the act of watching a loved one slowly deteriorate does to the psyche and the soul. The resulting exhaustion is both mental and physical, and for me, was coupled with the belief that no end was in sight. To hope for a light at the end of the tunnel, so to speak, was to think of that light as my mom's death, a thought that was way too conflicting. And, I already had more conflict than I could handle with Mia's continued decline.

With Mom, I protected myself by contending that my life, as it was at that moment, was how it would be into the indefinite future. Life after my mother was not a fathomable concept. How could it be? To plan my future meant planning on her dying. She couldn't die. She had become my daily source of love and affection.

• • •

Perhaps the overwhelming urge to be physically closer to Mom was a subconscious solution to offset the growing cognitive distance between us. Or, perhaps it was an answer to having to make the impossible daily decision between visiting her and rushing home to medicate Mia. Maybe some part of my brain that I refused to acknowledge or accept knew she was dying. It was probably all of these, I don't know. I don't recall thinking any of that. At the time, I just knew I needed to move her closer to my home.

Parkside was located less than three miles from my home and specialized in caring for Alzheimer's patients. The entire facility was secure, leaving a much larger safe space for the residents to walk and socialize than Hilltop Manor. The move also assured she would receive assistance with eating as necessary. Mom was able to handle utensils and feed herself on some days. Other days, she just couldn't seem to put the hand-utensil-mouth connection together and resorted to using her fingers.

Despite my strong feelings and the obvious benefits, it was a difficult decision to move Mom from where she had been happy and comfortable for so many years. I was again faced with having to weigh my concern for my mother against the unknown physical costs. Plus, the other Hilltop Manor residents and the caregivers were dear to me and had become part of my daily life. Regardless of how exhausted, unhappy or frustrated I felt before walking through the secured doors into the memory unit, the smiles, hugs, and kind gestures of the residents and caregivers always comforted me. I had come to know all the residents' personalities, their quirks, their likes and dislikes. I had participated with them in sing-alongs, chair exercises, memory games, and dances. Like my mother, many were left with only their true and beautiful spirits. The sparkles in their eyes were constant, their hugs sincere, their giggles genuine, and I loved them all.

In late February 2011, I met Parkside's administrator and head nurse for a facility tour, and then returned two days later and selected the room where (the recesses of my mind knew) Mom would spend her last days. I signed the necessary paperwork, and paid a deposit to hold a lovely single room overlooking an interior courtyard and flower gardens.

The following evening, a Friday, I arrived home from work to find Mia lying in her usual spot, except her back was to me, with no wagging of her tail. She turned her head around as I approached. She was sad, as if she couldn't be there for me the way she wanted, like she knew she was dying and was ashamed of it. She wasn't sorry for herself, she was sorry for me, and it broke my heart.

She perked up with the arrivals of Trey and Meredith and ate as usual. Lindsey came over to spend the night and we were all together as a family again. When I first arrived at home, I believed it was Mia's time to pass, but she decided otherwise. Trey and the girls walked her, and she played with renewed vigor and spirit. Lindsey stayed over again Saturday night, and while Mia still needed some assistance, she found strength in being a family.

When we awoke Sunday morning, something was different again. Mia was no longer able to get her feet underneath her to stand. All she could manage was to lift her head and gaze at us – her expression of disappointing us was now mixed with fear. No more questioning, all aligned and agreed it was time. I had been the stoic one, so after two painful attempts to pick Mia up, I drove to the veterinarian's office alone. On a recent visit the vet had offered the use of their transfer board if necessary to transport Mia to their office. It was now necessary.

As I approached the clinic's counter I recognized the clerk as one who knew Mia. A young father stood with his son at the end of the counter. The boy held the leash of a puppy, and the three appeared to be waiting for something from the clerk. She asked them to wait a minute and stepped toward me. "May I help you?"

I opened my mouth but nothing came out. I stood there with my mouth gaping, trying to speak the words – *what words?* I had no words. Right there in front of the clerk, the young father, his son, and their puppy, I just started bawling.

The clerk escorted me into an examining room and the vet came in soon after with the transfer board. She explained how best to move Mia with as little pain as possible. She also described the procedure for putting Mia to rest and said we could bring her in the late afternoon as they were closing to allow more time to say goodbye.

We all sat with Mia as the vet administered the drugs that took away her suffering. Trey, Lindsey, Meredith, and I stroked her fluffy white coat while looking into her ebony eyes and told her we loved her and how grateful we were she had chosen us. And then she was gone. The gleaming lights that had always shone in her eyes so brightly, even in her last days, had gone out.

• • •

My appointment with the creepy oral surgeon, Dr. Christopher, came two days after Mia's passing. Being told that I have two tumors in my face was the exclamation point-end of a five-day streak of heartbreaks.

I left Dr. Christopher's office in a daze and with an appointment card listing the time and location for the appointment with an ENT. Using a pencil, I had written "parotid" on the back of it after enlisting the nurse's help with spelling, and "Kaye" after asking her for the name of the DFW Metro doctor, the guy who had to *accept* me.

I ate lunch on the drive back to work. I was supposed to participate in staff training that included taking the Meyers-Briggs personality test, but decided it probably wasn't a good time to have my personality analyzed so I skipped out of the training and continued with my work.

I don't recall when I told Trey about the appointment. I also don't recall telling my daughters. One or two weeks passed. We were still mourning Mia, so I may not have wanted to worry them. Initially, I only shared the news with my boss because I had to leave work the next day for the ENT appointment. I made light of the situation as if I wasn't worried. I don't recall what I felt. I just kept moving forward.

By this time, my office was located in the executive suite and the view was to the west overlooking the Bullock State History Museum and the southwestern corner of the University of Texas campus. I had collected quotes and various words of inspiration and taped them to the wall around my computer monitor for encouragement.

"Forward Progress Always!"

Those were my words; just one of my many mantras at the time. Another was, *"Music is My Medicine!"* In the evenings after leaving my mother and Hilltop Manor, I blasted KGSR radio or a favorite CD to replenish my soul as I worked my way onto MoPac and crawled northward along with 50 million other cars.

I'd check out and let the music carry me home.

PART TWO

NOT SPEAKING YOUR TRUTH

When we disrespect our truths
we sublimate our power, and
essentially, our Selves

Chapter 6
YOU'RE NOT SPECIAL

I liked the ENT. Dr. Kelleigh was energetic, efficient, had a strong voice, and got to the point. She did not believe the bump in my cheek was malignant, but she thought it needed to be removed. She ordered a CT scan and set another appointment to get the results and draw fluid to biopsy. I told her about the other potential issue with my right condyle, and she assured me it would be covered in the CT scan report.

The report confirmed the bump in my right cheek was a small tumor in the parotid gland, and also increased Dr. Kelleigh's confidence that the tumor was not malignant. Nothing was listed in the report about my right condyle, no mention of my jaw whatsoever.

I pointed this out to Dr. Kelleigh. "Does this mean there is nothing wrong with my jaw?"

She glanced at the report again, stepped out to call the radiologist who had read the CT scan, and returned soon after. "He's going to take another look at the images and submit an amended report if necessary."

"Thank you."

She stuck a needle in my cheek and drew fluid for testing. Due to spring break, I had to wait two weeks for the results of the needle biopsy and to learn if something was going on with my right TMJ. I stayed occupied with work and moving Mom, and adopted a mindset that Dr. Christopher's x-rays must have been wrong.

Due to a prior experience with a false-positive x-ray shadow, rather than thinking a radiologist had committed such a huge oversight, it was more plausible to believe the CT scan had provided a clearer picture and revealed no growth on my right condyle. Which is why I refused to schedule an appointment when Dr. Kaye's office called the following week. Yes, I had been accepted. That isn't what the scheduling clerk stated; she was just following instructions to book an appointment and seemed a little confused by my contention that I didn't need one. I agreed to take down her name and number and promised to call her back if anything changed.

Somehow the radiologist had missed the fact that the top of my right jaw had stretched upward and curled inward, and looked like a bent pinky finger. *How the fuck does someone miss that!*

The needle biopsy provided another level of assurance the parotid gland tumor was benign; however, only by removing the tumor could that diagnosis be one hundred percent affirmed. This required removing the entire top layer of the parotid gland. Dr. Kelleigh was ready to schedule surgery, but with confirmation of a bone tumor in the same area, she accepted my preference for both tumors to be treated at the DFW Metro Medical Center.

My thinking was one of efficiency. I was bargaining for a two-for-one surgery so I could minimize both the pain and time out of my life. Dr. Kelleigh agreed, but later called to assure I had contacted DFW Metro and the parotid gland tumor would be removed. Maybe she had sensed my annoyance and impatience with having to deal with medical issues. Before leaving her office, I had also concluded that any such surgery could wait two months until the end of the Texas Legislative Session. I did not share this decision with her or anyone else, but rather made sure that would be the case through my actions, or rather, inactions.

Between Mom's and my ongoing medical needs, I felt that I'd taken too much personal time, which only added to my stress. Those who work in or around the Texas Capitol and its legislative process know not to take off during the first five months of every odd year. If you get the flu, you work. If a friend dies, you go to the funeral only if you can get there and back in a day.

Not that the entire legislative process, or even my office, would have come tumbling down if I missed a couple of weeks at work. Not even close. Yet, with all the added responsibilities and life stresses, I performed my job with even more dedication and determination. *Why?*

I don't know; a certain urgency seemed to always permeate my body, a vigilance driven by something in another time. All my work environments had offered me acceptance, relevance and recognition. Yet, I continued to over perform, propelled by a desperate need to prove my worth and justify my existence, even to the point of exhaustion.

• • •

I unburied the blue sticky note from the credenza abutting my work desk. It was as I left it three-and-a-half weeks prior when the woman from DFW Metro Medical Center called to schedule an appointment. An appointment was set this time for the last week in April.

Although Trey accompanied me to the early morning appointment, the thought of heading out of town by myself appealed to me. I couldn't bring myself to tell Trey that I needed three hours to myself to think. Since it had not even occurred to me this would be a question, we also didn't discuss whether he would accompany me into the examining room. We had never encroached on each other's doctor appointments in the past. So when Trey made the offer, which was not until we sat in the waiting room while I filled out paperwork, he wasn't surprised by my response – a resounding "No."

I hadn't hurt his feelings. He knew me well enough to accept that I took care of myself and handled my own business. It was a kind gesture on his part, and he had a genuine and understandable concern for my welfare. I sensed he wanted to hear Dr. Kaye's opinion firsthand. However, at the time, Trey's escorting me would raise the matter to a level of concern I was not willing to acknowledge. Furthermore, it would be a false portrayal of an open and close relationship.

Neither of these were healthy perspectives, but they were my feelings at the time and should have been respected. Trey understood, and heeded to my position without objection. The problem came when the unsuspecting nurse opened the door into the waiting room and called my name. I rose alone and headed toward her. As I entered the doorway, I turned to wave at Trey. He responded with a smile that said, "Good luck," and waved back.

In a don't-be-ridiculous tone, the nurse said, "Honey, he can come with you!"

But, I don't want him to!

Dumbfounded, my gaze moved from the nurse back to Trey, who grinned with raised eyebrows as if asking, *What do you say?* He was also tickled at the platter of awkward I had been served. All eyes in the waiting room were on me as I stammered and then conceded to not be the bitch who didn't want the cute man, who obviously loved me, chaperon me into the vestibule of the unknown.

I waved him over. Trey appeared happy to have breached the confines of my personal world. I wasn't rude to him once we entered the examining room, but I wasn't exactly nice either. When the nurse noted my elevated blood pressure, I turned to him and said, in a half-joking tone for the benefit of the nurse, "See, you're stressing me out!"

Dr. Kaye soon entered and took charge. My first thought upon setting eyes on him was that the photo accompanying his online bio was dated. He was older than I had anticipated, but his mild, friendly, and slightly nerdy demeanor was consistent with my expectations.

Over the course of the next hour and a half, my face was measured and pressed upon, every facial orifice was examined, CT scan images were viewed and discussed, my medical history and parotid gland tumor were discussed, professional opinions were stated, and questions by all parties were asked and answered. He was taken aback by, and even questioned, why no doctor or dentist had pursued finding a reason behind the TMJ pain and other symptoms. I also had difficulty convincing him there was no previous injury to the area and he, like the medical professionals before him, quizzed me about grinding and clinching.

Fixing a steady gaze on me, he said, "Have you been particularly stressed?"

My face must have reflected the thoughts that overwhelmed my brain. Before I could sort and gather them, which took longer than it should have, Dr. Kaye pre-empted any response. "The price of gasoline is enough to stress anyone out."

He had given me an out. *The price of gasoline is the last thing I'm stressed about.*

Because I had no previous injury to the area, the suspected—and best possible—prognosis was an arthritic growth. A malignant tumor was not ruled out, but odds were in my favor, as I was outside the typical age range. Nothing would be known without a biopsy. Conducting a biopsy on the condyle required major surgery, so such masses are normally removed first and biopsied afterwards.

I asked, "Can the condyle mass be removed at the same time as the parotid tumor?"

With a sympathetic head shake Dr. Kaye replied, "No, not without causing too much trauma to the area."

Throughout the back-and-forth discussion, I didn't fully grasp that the mass, one way or another, would have to be removed. In what was probably an effort to pacify my reluctance to accept this, Dr. Kaye agreed to consult with the otorhinolaryngology department on coordinating a surgery to remove the parotid tumor and biopsy the condyle mass. A two-for-one compromise I could agree with, but that would not necessarily negate the need for another surgery.

The next step was to identify the nature of the mass through a bone scan. The scan followed protocol, but I got the impression it wasn't completely necessary based on the growth's size, my continued pain, and Dr. Kaye's comment. "I bet you light up like a Christmas tree."

Either way, a bone scan would confirm whether or not the mass was actively growing, and subsequently determine, at least in my mind, the need for its removal. I agreed to have a scan performed in Austin and have the results sent to him. As the nurse escorted us out of the examining room, I noticed the hours that had passed and asked her to thank Dr. Kaye for his patience.

More don't-be-ridiculous attitude, "You can thank him yourself, it's okay."

She led me to an office where he sat at a computer. He rose and shook my hand as I acknowledged the time he'd spent with me. How new and refreshing that someone in the medical field listened to—*and believed*—me. At last someone addressed the root cause of my pain, pain I had long accepted was the result of something I did.

• • •

My mother had been settled into her new residence for six weeks and the move proved to be helpful in allowing me to better monitor her eating and general care. There was also the added bonus of reducing the stress of my routine. The Parkside administrator had requested a meeting to provide a standard review of Mom's care. I put her off for longer than appropriate, but finally arranged the meeting for Friday, four days after my appointment with Dr. Kaye and the same afternoon the bone scan was scheduled.

The bone scan required two appointments – the first to inject a radioactive substance and then another four hours later to perform the imaging. The time gap was perfect for driving to Parkside for the meeting and minimizing my time away from work. *Efficiency*!

I arrived at Parkside with a bright blue surgical bandage around my arm, which, unless I lied, required an explanation about my face and how it might impact my availability in the near future. Not many people were privy to my medical issues. Primarily because I didn't know how to subtly convey the unknowns. Plus, I wanted the people around me to support my nonchalant attitude, my denial, but even vague explanations garnered annoying looks of concern.

Such was the case with the Parkside administrator and the head nurse who was unexpectedly present for the meeting. My news may have also tempered what was supposed to be a meeting to provide me with a reality check. The level of Mom's care had been established based on information I provided. She had since been moved from the main dining area and was receiving extra help getting to and eating all meals. She needed, and was receiving, the highest level of care – two full levels above what I had indicated. She functioned as a one year old, and I had thought she was three.

The nurse then brought up the subject of hospice and how they provided Medicare-approved services well before death was imminent. She added that hospice services also assist family members. "I'm sure Abigail will qualify, and I'm happy to make the arrangements if you are ready."

What I heard, though, was hospice would assist me in overseeing the care of my mother. I didn't think I needed help… receiving help was a sign of weakness, of failure. Nor did I accept that Mom required hospice care. I hadn't yet processed the fact that she required level-five care, and now they recommended hospice. A sense of uncertainty accompanied this news. The blanket of love and protection with which I had shielded her since the evening of my father's funeral had become tattered. I realized this for a brief moment as I sat before them and as my bones absorbed radioactive material.

They were confronting my denial with compassion and sensitivity. They were offering to help, but I was not ready to relinquish my control. My sense of control, and Mom's affection, were what held me together.

I thanked the nurse and declined. "I promise to let you know if I change my mind."

After a brief visit with Mom and hugs from her and some of the residents, I headed back into Austin for the bone scan.

• • •

The radiological tech was friendly and we had established good rapport earlier in the day when she shot me up with radioactive material. "Am I glowing enough now?"

We laughed and engaged in chummy chatter throughout the scan, but alas her professionalism was firmly entrenched. She refused to divulge what she had seen on the scan image. In compensation, she shared, "The radiologist will review the image later today, and you can order a copy of it and the report on Monday."

Deal!

The image would reveal whether the mass on my condyle needed to be removed. That question begged for an answer; I wanted some insight as to what was in store for me. I didn't want my face to be cut open twice and was glad only the weekend stood between me and the next decision.

After work the following Monday, I stopped by the radiological office on my way to Parkside. A brown manila envelope waited for me at the counter. I opened it in my car and scanned the report, hoping it would not include the word "active." But active was there, looming just behind the word metabolically. As Dr. Kaye had expected, the mass was still growing.

I brushed aside the tinge of disappointment – *Forward Progress Always!* – slipped the report back into the manila envelope, placed it in the passenger seat, blasted the radio, and headed to Mom's. Music subdued my internal chaos until I arrived. Mom had become an unlimited source of comfort, hugs, and love, despite her not knowing why I needed her, or even perhaps who I was.

Once home, I popped the compact disc into my computer and pulled up the bone scan image. Dr. Kaye was correct. In the area of my right ear was a round white circle the size of a quarter with a fuzzy bright glow, just like a light on a Christmas tree.

• • •

Before the two-for-one surgery could be scheduled, I had to become an established patient with Dr. Abbey, the DFW Metro ENT who would perform the parotidectomy.

Following the precedence set by Dr. Kaye's nurse, Trey accompanied me into the examining room. I didn't mind so much this time. The vestibule was known, the level of concern somewhat acknowledged, and I would be relying on Trey for post-surgical care. I needed him.

Dr. Abbey was quick and concise. I gave her copies of the CT images and the report that the Austin ENT had ordered, along with the biopsy pathology report. She poked around the area of the parotid gland tumor, which had grown even larger and more painful. She was satisfied enough to move forward with coordinating her and Dr. Kaye's schedules for the dual surgeries.

• • •

The first pre-operative appointment started with more medical history questions from a resident surgeon. He seemed anxious, which I thought was odd, and the questioning covered areas irrelevant to my jaw. The relevant information came later from Dr. Kaye, who first informed me that Dr. Abbey would be the lead surgeon. He added, "And that's okay," as if being secondary was something he'd grown to accept.

She would perform the parotidectomy first, and then he and his team would take over and perform the condyle biopsy. The combined surgeries would take about three hours.

"How are you going to take the biopsy sample? Are you going to scrape, bore, or—"

"Yes."

I did not follow exactly what Dr. Kaye said from that point, but left with a general understanding that his team was prepared to evaluate whatever they found and take whatever action was feasible. I was told not to be surprised if I awoke from the anesthesia with brackets on my teeth and my mouth wired shut.

Dr. Abbey gave a clear explanation of what the parotidectomy would entail. She confirmed what I had discovered via "Dr. Google" was current as far as the procedure and healing time. The greatest risk was damage to the facial nerve that intersects the parotid gland. If the nerve was harmed during the surgery, my face muscles would droop – Bell's palsy.

Dr. Abbey's description of the order of the procedures was consistent with Dr. Kaye's, except she added she would return following the biopsy to suture the incision. The incision was to start at my hairline just above and in front of my right ear, continue down my face bordering the front of my ear, weave around and behind the earlobe, and then curve downward into my neck a couple of inches following the jawline.

• • •

After I had been prepped for the OR, I met Dr. Kennedy, who was to assist with the first surgery. I had just made the skimpy standard-issue hospital gown less skimpy with a couple of pieces of surgical tape. The inch-long slit used for inserting tubes had been gaping open as if it had been overstretched. The slit fell directly over my left breast, providing a perfectly sized hole for my nipple. Who knew how long it had been like that? Trey hadn't noticed; but the anesthesiologist who stopped by my pre-op room earlier had made a sudden and quick exit. I noticed the wardrobe malfunction immediately after he left.

"Fuck!" I fetched the tape from a nearby medical tray to prevent any more peep shows, and hoped I would be unconscious during my next encounter with the anesthesiologist.

Dr. Kennedy didn't notice the tape. She was young and had entered the room with her purse over her shoulder and a Starbucks cup in hand. She reviewed paperwork, asked me questions, pressed the lump in my cheek, and marked my neck with a felt-tipped pen without really looking at me or setting down her coffee and purse. I felt like a piece of furniture.

She wasn't out of sorts or stressed like she'd had a bad morning. She was just rude, as if her behavior were deliberate. It bothered me, and as she left Trey and I caught each other's eyes and our eyebrows lifted in unison as if to say, *Wow, that was weird!*

We ended up laughing. "What was that?"

• • •

A male voice interrupted a sublime dream from the vantage point of being on the sideline of a lush green pitch with colorful uniformed soccer players. "She's waking up."

Someone else commented about stable blood pressure – probably the anesthesiologist I had nip-slipped. My prevailing concern however was, *has my mouth been wired shut?* I guided my tongue between my teeth and ran it across the front of them... *Another surgery.*

One question answered. The next answer came later from Dr. Kaye, "Confidence is high the condylar mass is benign."

His persona had transformed. He beamed while discussing the potential diagnosis of Unilateral Condylar Hyperplasia. A rare condition, it had not been listed as a possibility during previous appointments, and this was good news. The mass appeared to be bone. My right condyle, without explanation, was growing and had been for at least the past five years. I was also grateful to learn my facial nerve had survived the procedure unscathed.

While being wheeled to a regular hospital room, I was alert enough to keep an eye out for Trey. I hoped to see him at some point. *He must be waiting in my room.* Upon entering the sullen sterility of my room, I lifted my head and scanned its perimeter, *not here.*

The surgeries had taken five hours, and I had been out of recovery for an hour before Trey was informed. He insisted the mishap was the fault of the waiting room clerk and not because he was consumed by his work.

Although suspect of Trey's rendition of the waiting room events, I was still glad for his presence. He stayed with me, holding my hand, well into the evening as I drifted in and out. His hand had to be cramping as it draped over the bed railing. Yet, he continued holding mine, and I felt comforted through the gesture. We hadn't experienced that degree of closeness for some time.

Assuring him that I was fine and promising to call if anything was needed, I convinced Trey to return to the hotel around 10:00 p.m. The morphine pump was keeping me pain free and feeling cozy. I pushed its 'go' button every time I noticed the light indicating sufficient time had passed. I continued this routine through the night despite—or perhaps because I was—feeling pretty darn good.

The effects of maintaining a morphine buzz caught up with me by daybreak. Nausea awakened me, followed by heaves of stomach fluid mixed with bile. Within minutes, Dr. Kennedy arrived and after chiding the nurse cleaning me up, she dismantled the morphine pump. That, and a shot of Phenergan, took care of my stomach, and over the course of the next couple of hours, I felt better and ready to eat, or rather drink. I was restricted to liquids for 24 hours.

When breakfast rolled around, I turned away the liquid options offered in anticipation of the fruit smoothie Trey had promised. That is how I had started each day over the past year.

Trey and I biologically existed in different time zones (pacific and eastern, respectively), which could cause conflicts and delays. Plus, Trey had a habit of working into the early morning hours. This possibility should have occurred to me as his 2:00 a.m. emails were notorious among his staff and co-workers. When Trey appeared in the late morning, I had gone too long without food, and the grape slushy he offered wasn't the sustenance I wanted and needed.

Soon after, Dr. Abbey arrived and removed the tape covering my incision and a drainage tube from my neck. Her instruction to keep the stitched incision uncovered was unsettling and I was only marginally pacified by the tube of antibacterial ointment she handed me.

I sat on the hospital bed sipping my grape slushy awaiting Dr. Kaye's arrival and my official discharge. The wait provided time to relay an earlier experience to Trey and the clarity to get pissed off about it. While in recovery the previous afternoon, I'd noticed pressure being applied around the lower half of my legs. Later I realized the cause was a set of air compression sleeves. Although used to prevent blood clots, I had not expected to need them. Most everything I experienced up to that point had been anticipated based on the details provided by all the doctors, nurses, and medical techs. No one had discussed air compression sleeves.

Prior to the surgery, I had been concerned about the risk of blood clots because I had been working 10- to 12-hour shifts in the waning days of, and in the weeks following, the legislative session. Most of my time was spent sitting down at a computer. This alone was a risk for blood clots, but I did not raise the question prior to surgery. You see, when one is a patient, any assertiveness possessed in regular life can get checked at the door. Questions get rated in order of importance, and only those deemed relevant to absolute survival get posed.

Clearheaded the morning following the surgery, I wondered whether I should have mentioned my worry. Maybe something had caused a concern during the surgery, or perhaps compression pumps were standard procedure? I had attempted to ask Dr. Kennedy this, but she cut me off in a condescending tone. "Oh no, you're not special."

Her words deflated my lungs, resonated through my body and stirred something vaguely familiar. Shame. Shame in who I was, and shame in my existence. I didn't know how to respond except to say, "Okay, thank you."

After a longer-than-necessary pause, she'd added, "We do that for everyone."

Waiting with Trey, I was fuming. "I wasn't asking if I was special! Why would she think that?"

Trey shrugged. "I'm sure she didn't mean it that way."

"Why would she say it? Even if the air compression sleeves weren't protocol, they certainly didn't make me feel special while stuck in a hospital bed with an IV in my arm, a drainage bulb hanging out of my neck, and a fresh five-inch scar running down the side of my face!"

Dr. Kennedy had spent a total of ten minutes with me over two occasions, and in both instances she had successfully conveyed her belief that my existence was inconsequential. Her cadence and words, "you're not special," stung for some time as I wondered, and somewhat obsessed over, what compelled her behavior.

What annoyed her? Why did she take it out on me?

Is it just me, or does she treat all her patients that way?

Chapter 7
THE PROMISE

The 200-mile drive on Interstate 35 between Austin and Dallas-Ft. Worth is rarely pleasant under the best of circumstances, and the Hydrocodone tablets were no substitute for morphine. In order to lessen the effects of Trey's tendency to avoid braking until absolutely necessary, I surrounded myself with pillows for the return drive.

Neither biopsy report was available when I returned for the one-week post-operative appointments, but both would eventually confirm the tumors were benign. Dr. Abbey removed the stitches and instructed me to continue applying antibacterial ointment to the incision and leave it uncovered. She required no further follow-up appointments. Pleased with this news, I was happy to say good-bye to her and her staff.

The follow-up with Dr. Kaye focused on the function of my jaw. Eating was the primary topic and apparently some communication gap had occurred between him and Dr. Abbey. I had been told in the hospital to switch from liquids to soft foods after 24 hours. I ate a cheese enchilada and refried beans soon after being discharged; a baked sweet potato on the drive to Austin; and fish and eggs had since been my daily sources of protein.

Trey's eyes homed in on me as I sat wide-eyed and maintained innocence while Dr. Kaye rattled off soft foods to add to my diet, all of which I had already eaten. He finished with foods I could transition to over various time periods, ending with hamburgers and hotdogs.

Hotdogs? I know what to eat; you don't need to tell me.

Dr. Kaye detected my annoyance and mumbled something about Type

A personalities before moving onto the next steps. In three weeks, I would need another CT scan to provide a three-dimensional image of my jaw and face. I didn't have a clear understanding of what the next surgical step would entail and didn't ask for clarification. I had consulted Dr. Google on Condylar Hyperplasia, but the information I found was either dated or in pay-per-article medical journals. The most consistent corrective procedure referenced was a "condylectomy," which sounded simple enough. I had just undergone a parotidectomy, which went well and took care of the problem.

After the appointment, I waited for Trey in an atrium area while he purchased caffeine for the drive to Austin. As I waited, my eyes met Dr. Kaye's, who appeared to be leaving the building in a rush. We acknowledged each other with a smile, and he turned to approach me.

He made some comment about safe travels, and I noted that I was not looking forward to the drive. He gleamed as he shared news that "our youngest son" had been accepted to the University of Texas at Austin, and "we're very proud."

Dr. Kaye would soon be making that drive regularly, too – we had something in common. I responded with sincerity and enthusiasm. "Admittance into UT Austin is no easy feat. You should be proud!"

The brief conversation ended with his joke, "Perhaps I'll have to make a home visit!"

I laughed and responded, "Yes, absolutely," and he turned and headed with his fast pace toward the exit.

• • •

I waited ten days after the surgery to visit Mom at Parkside. I'm not generally a germaphobe, but it seemed risky to expose the healing incision to the residents' hugs and hands. I attempted to return to work after two weeks, which was the timeframe approved by Dr. Abbey. Still in a lot of pain, I felt weak, and my coworkers were apprehensive about the exposed scar but welcomed me. I lasted two-and-a-half days.

I needed to send an email to let friends know we couldn't attend their August wedding in England. Trey was to be the best man, and the flights had been booked six months prior. He did not want to attend without me, and I knew I would not be up to the trip.

Plus, I had a strong intuition I shouldn't go. Tears streamed down my face while drafting the email – I felt terrible about cancelling. I felt terrible, period. In an attempt to contain my emotions, I decided to get out for lunch.

While backing out of my parking space, I had to strain to move the steering wheel left. As I eased down on the accelerator my Tribute traveled only straight back. Its steering was out, I had lost control over which direction I wished to travel – the perfect analogy of my life at the time, and for some time to come.

After heading back inside, I took the elevator to my office and called a tow truck. Exhausted and in pain, I had held back too much emotion for too long. The dam broke as I closed my office door. I was done, and sent my boss an email telling her about my car and included the comment, "I hate my life right now."

She called me soon after and suggested I take the remainder of the week off. I was grateful for the reprieve. I needed more time.

As I wrote in my journal:

> "My meltdown was very much needed, past due, and therefore, therapeutic. It's not that I haven't consciously dealt with my ongoing medical issues, but I have avoided the emotions that would naturally accompany what I am going through – instead, forcing tears and any feelings of self-pity aside … "it could be worse… hey, it's not cancer." "So many people have it much worse, etc., etc." Even now, the most appropriate word I can find is "self-pity," yet

recognizing my very usage of that particular noun is a continuation of my discounting my own situation. I don't think all women have these conflicting thoughts, but most do, maybe.

At any rate, I finally allowed myself to cry, to feel sad that this is happening. As Meredith pointed out, life is a road sign – "Warning! Steep Grades and Sharp Curves Ahead!" I'm ready for some smooth, straight roadways but will navigate the roads laid before me the best I can. I pray that I do so with grace, patience, goodness and energy, and am thankful I've made it this far."

I had no idea of what lay ahead for me.

• • •

Sometime over my 10-day absence from Parkside, Mom was placed on a soft food diet. She consumed the same food, just blended. She had also become confined to a wheelchair by this time, which made getting her to and from doctor and dentist appointments more challenging.

Our weekend outings were now limited to brunch or dinner at my house. I attempted to engage her on detour treks around the southwestern shore of Lake Travis, but I'm not sure how much she took in. She had once delighted at the sight of wildflowers lining the roads. Now it was difficult to even get her attention.

As July wore on through a record-breaking heat wave, the pain in my right cheek and jaw remained constant. Visits with Mom became even more of a refuge while my workload continued at a legislative session pace and Trey's and my relationship remained in its comfortable rut. I'd help her eat, clean her up, and then wheel her around the hallways surrounding the atrium. We'd end up at a window in the library, her room, or a hallway where we could look out into the garden. I pointed out plants, flowers, birds, and an occasional butterfly. Afterwards, we'd park in the living area where the other high-need residents gathered to watch an old movie. I sat on a stool next to her and leaned the pain-free side of my face onto her arm while holding her hand.

She couldn't talk but she was there for me. On evenings I worked late, I arrived in time to help her change for bed, my preferred time to visit. I kept a few record albums in her room and played them on her "Victrola" – that is what she always called it. It was a turntable, radio, and CD player built into a tall, four-legged, Victorian-style, oak cabinet that she and Dad had ordered from a catalog ten years earlier.

Mom had never been much of a music fan; not like Dad, anyway. So, I selected only a few albums I was fairly confident she would enjoy. *Music from Doctor Zhivago*, Paul Mauriat's *Mauriat Magic*, and a compilation cover album entitled, *Honey and Other Greatest Hits*, which included cheesy but awesome songs such as "Daydream Believer," "Do You Know the Way to San Jose," and "Everlasting Love."

Music is a time machine transporting one into memories. The melodies, voices, and lyrics of these albums induced my childhood senses of comfort and the innocent naiveté of all existing perfect in the world. They evoked the happy memories of living in the small, modest house on Westward Street in Wichita Falls. It had wooden floors and old white steel kitchen appliances at a time when one's financial and social statuses were exhibited through shag carpet and harvest gold appliances.

The songs conjured images of Mom wearing a bright yellow double-knit pantsuit with white accent pockets that she had sewn and seemed to be happy and confident while wearing; and memories of exotic dinners, such as Hawaiian chicken with cashews or sautéed kidneys over toasted French bread that she prepared from the *Joy of Cooking*. The smooth melodies of Paul Mauriat played as we ate these savory meals by the light of a candle stuck in a wine bottle so its wax melted down the bottle's sides.

When the candle melted to a stub, we'd replace it with another candle of a different color until there were layers and layers of multicolored wax drippings built up around the bottleneck. When the wax buildup was big enough, we started the process again with another bottle until we had a matching set of colorful wine bottle candelabras. They were beautiful.

Most childhood memories of my mother are from the perspective of observation rather than engagement. I saw her. She was fun, smart, strong, opinionated, and on the go. While operating a daycare business out of our home, she and Dad had enrolled in Wichita Falls' local state college when I was three. I'm not sure how they handled both the business and schoolwork, but I do recall always falling asleep to the sound of a busy Smith-Corona.

Our little Westward house was alive with the culture of the late 1960's as reflected in my parents' literature, art, music, food, and friends. A few years after my parents graduated college and had been teaching, they covered its wooden floors with multi-colored gold, orange, and yellow shag carpet and put it up for sale.

One summer in the early 1970's, we moved to a large ranch-style home in a more prestigious neighborhood. The first night we spent in the new house, I lay with my sister on a pallet in our new bedroom and cried myself to sleep. Things were going to be different from that point, I could feel it. On Westward Street the world was small, manageable for a young benevolently neglected girl. It contained my soul's resources, those things and places where I gained senses of comfort, safety, and belonging.

In the new house and neighborhood, I was forced into reality. I felt alone, and even less relevant... *the new house was special.* Our large stereo cabinet was relegated to the patio and replaced with a console color television. Its turntable and speakers were removed and the empty space instead held a kelly-green plastic dishware set for outdoor meals. The old record albums were stored, and the wine bottle candelabras were thrown away.

Just as all that was good in the sixties evolved into whatever the seventies were, the magic of my childhood also faded.

Through the music I played while resting with Mom in her room, I was happily transported to the time living on Westward Street. One evening as I lay next to her feeling particularly exhausted and tired of the pain throbbing throughout the right side of my face, I confessed all my worries. I sought solace and she was my only trusted confidant.

My emotions flowed as I told her how I felt overwhelmed, afraid, and unsure how I was going to be able to handle the next surgery. I confided in her because I needed a mother, and because I didn't think I had anyone else. In every other aspect of my life, my role was the grounded stalwart force keeping the worlds spinning, and in those worlds, I didn't know how to be anything else.

• • •

When it was measured at the one-month post-surgical appointment, the degree to which I could open my mouth had decreased to about the width of my index finger. Dr. Kaye explained if the mass were not removed, my jaw would eventually fuse shut and I would not be able to eat.

I was already limited on what I could eat. Anything wider than my mouth opening required smashing down to fit through my teeth. To avoid awkwardness at social and work-related meals, I made light of that fact by stating I was on a "flat-food diet," and only ordered foods that easily fit into my mouth. That pretty much limited me to soup, pizza, and chalupas.

Dr. Kaye also explained that the three-dimensional image would be used to create custom molded prostheses to reconstruct my TMJ joint. He would send the image to a "California company" that would take six to eight weeks to build the titanium, chromium, nickel, and plastic parts that would be set in my mandible with titanium screws to form a new and functioning joint.

Previously he had referred to the "California company," and I wondered why he did not call it by its name, like it was some clandestine entity, or maybe he felt he needed to keep terminology to a fourth grade level.

I did comprehend the seriousness of the situation. I just didn't like it. With the understanding that all systems were go on ordering the prostheses, I left the appointment and headed home to Austin. Perhaps another miscommunication had occurred, because I was surprised to receive a phone call from Dr. Kaye sometime afterward. Before approving the construction of the prostheses and scheduling a surgery date, he wanted to make sure the device was what I wanted.

I stammered with confusion. It had never occurred to me that I had a choice in the matter. My jaw was fusing shut, and I was in constant pain! Another surgery was not what I wanted, but I was under the impression it was necessary. Did he need my approval or was he asking me, *Are you sure you really want to do this?*

This perception, or misperception, made me question whether the surgery was truly needed and in my confusion I couldn't answer the question. Instead, I turned the question around. "What would you do?"

Without having to think twice, I had made major medical decisions for my mother. I had always known what to do when it came to her care, but in response to a simple, and probably procedural, question related to my own health, I relinquished all rational thought and my power.

Dr. Kaye recommended I have the surgery. Once I conceded, he informed me it would take place around late September or early October.

• • •

While at work mid-morning on Monday, August 1st, I received a phone call from an assistant nurse at Parkside. Mom had not wanted to get up for breakfast and was drifting in and out of sleep. She wasn't running a fever nor appeared to be ill, he'd just wanted to let me know and would continue monitoring her.

Based on his assurance, I continued with my day and called to check on Mom in the early afternoon. The report was the same – they were regularly checking on her and she was in good spirits while awake, but she would not get out of bed.

I already had plans to leave work early for an annual eye exam. The eye appointment was quick and routine, and I was happy to run into Tracy there. I had not seen her since moving Mom out of Hilltop Manor where we would often visit during lunch and dinner hours. Her mother and Mom had been roommates and got along well. Tracy and I lived with the same daily challenges, and I had missed having authentic conversations about those challenges with someone who truly understood them. Before leaving to check on Mom, we exchanged quick updates and wished each other well.

As I was buzzed into Parkside's living area, the evening assistant nurse met me. On the way to Mom's room, she recapped what the male nurse had stated and stood with me as I roused Mom to say hello. She opened her eyes and a wide and enthusiastic smile came over her face. She seemed to know who I was and attempted to rise as her arms reached for a hug. She appeared joyful in a way I'd never seen her before and then slipped immediately back into a slumber.

The nurse then motioned me into the hallway. She shared the head nurse's opinion that Mom's condition would not change. "Would you like me to contact hospice?"

I agreed, and now see in hindsight that the nurses and care associates had been as attentive and considerate of me as they had been for Mom.

Within an hour, Meredith showed up, as did a hospice representative. This was the first time I heard the term "active dying state." I didn't like it. The word "active" implied Mom was choosing to die, but the hospice representative explained it was a decision of her body – a natural shutting down process that could take from one day to two weeks.

She measured Mom's oxygen level and examined her legs and back, looking for mottling. She found none, and then described the discolorations that would appear like blotches under Mom's skin, usually beginning on the legs.

When she moved to Austin seven years prior, Mom had signed both a Medical Power of Attorney and a Do Not Resuscitate Order. Parkside had copies of both and shared them with the hospice representative. Despite the DNR order, I was given the option to have a feeding tube inserted into Mom's stomach. Mom would not want one, but the predominant thought that had me refusing was a deep desire for her to remain as comfortable, peaceful, and pain-free as possible. No way would I allow anyone to cut her in any form or fashion. I just wanted to take care of her, protect her, and keep her comfortable and feeling safe.

Finally, the representative went over a list of services that hospice would provide. She said she would return in the morning, but a general hospice nurse would begin overseeing Mom's care and monitoring her condition from that point. She left me with a plastic bag holding the contents that were to sustain my mother's life for the next day or two, or ten. *Who knows?* Her death was another unpredictable certainty in our seven-year journey together.

I fumbled through the bag and retrieved a lip balm along with a handful of plastic blue sticks with small pointed sponges. I dipped the sponge end of one of the sticks into a small cup of water and used it to moisten Mom's cracked lips and hydrate her tongue and mouth. She reacted innately, just as an infant would.

Trey and Lindsey arrived in the early evening with dinner. After we ate, the girls stayed with Mom while I made a quick trip home for a change of clothes and toiletries. I also grabbed a couple of down comforters and pillows, and called both of my brothers. I had no idea if Mom would make it through the night or for another week, so I promised to keep them updated.

That evening, Meredith slept on the floor at the foot of Mom's bed, and I lay with Mom. She was positioned on the right side of her bed so this required lying on my painful side in order to face her. I spent most the night upright, assuring her lips and tongue stayed moist. She remained peaceful and seemed to be comfortable.

I waited until the next morning to contact Susan. She and her husband had reached Bali, Indonesia, readying their sailboat for the remaining voyage around the world. Over the next five days, she and my brothers would make their ways to Austin and to Mom's side.

As the days and nights merged into one, I lost all sense of time. I stayed with Mom around the clock, while Lindsey and Meredith traded nights sleeping on the floor, and Trey kept us supplied with food and fresh clothes. I fed her ice until she stopped responding to it, kept her lips and tongue moistened, combed her hair, checked her legs for mottling, and assured she was kept clean and comfortable.

The afternoon that Trey and I had been scheduled to fly to England, I sat alone with Mom while thinking about her life and spirited personality. Once during my teen years, she had opened up during a driving trip to Oklahoma and confided that she had aspired to be a foreign news correspondent. She was in high school during World War II, and traveling and reporting on world events had seemed glamorous.

As I held her hand, I imagined a young, vibrant version of Abigail jotting words into a reporter's notebook on the streets of 1940's London. I ached for her unrealized dream, the life she'd wanted, and I wondered if she had other regrets. Leaning into her, I whispered, "Mom, I promise you that I will live my life fully."

It seemed like a way to honor her true self… the one she had sacrificed.

Mom never appeared to be in pain, but the weekend hospice nurse started her on regular doses of morphine. This hospice nurse was older and spoke with a stern Irish accent.

By Saturday, all siblings arrived and gathered around her bed to say their goodbyes. We sat in her room all afternoon, catching up through boisterous conversations ranging in topics as varied as our personalities. Until, that is, the hospice nurse asked if she could speak to me.

I stepped into the hallway and followed her around a corner. My sister noticed and followed, and my brothers trailed my sister. The nurse looked at me and in her stern Irish accent asked me if my mother had been a private person. I did not have to think on this – there was no question that she was, and always had been. I nodded.

"If she was a private person before, that hasn't changed. She is still a private person."

She placed her hand on my shoulder. "You're not letting her go, dear. Your mum may be waiting for you all to leave."

Six days earlier, when the hospice rep had explained what was needed, my "marching orders" were clear. I had rolled up my sleeves and proceeded to become the stalwart force in control of my mom's world.

The Irish nurse had held up a mirror in front of me. She was right. I would relinquish my control over to Mom and the Universe and allow her the peace and solitude she had always loved. I tidied up her room and kissed her cheek. Her face had sunken over the course of the last six days and her arms and legs seemed fragile, but she was still beautiful. "I love you, Mom. I'll see you tomorrow."

I faced the setting sun as I pulled out of Parkside's parking lot alone and reached for the radio – a couple of seconds of silence passed before Patty Griffin's voice belted out the words, "Oh, heavenly day."

"Heavenly Day" is an amazing song about optimism, gratitude, and embracing life and its beauty. I don't know why it always took music to loosen the concrete burying my emotions. Music knows my soul. It knows how to break me when I need breaking, and heal me when I need healing.

That evening, after seeing Mom for the last time, the voice, music, and lyrics of Patty Griffin did both.

Chapter 8
THE SEED OF GRATITUDE

Following mom's passing, my home became a gathering place for my siblings and extended family, and the conversations and commotion recommenced. None knew what my soul had endured the last seven years with mom… they had not lived with the daily stress, the worry, the unpredictability. My siblings didn't carry seven years of repressed heartache and angst because they hadn't had to show up for mom every day with a smile on their face. I'm sure they carried something, but we'd never been taught to show our pain, much less discuss it.

My body was exhausted and my mind emotionally exasperated. I needed sleep. I needed to breathe, and I needed to grieve. Instead of calmly conveying this, I lost it and demanded that everyone leave.

I spent the next morning on my backyard patio all to myself. I didn't grieve. I didn't think about much of anything. I just sat there listening to the birds and enjoying the heat of the sun on my face. When it became too hot, I met Trey and Lindsey for a late lunch and then headed to a department store where—perhaps in an attempt to fill a void—I spent $300 on clothes I didn't need.

My siblings and I did not discuss the subject of planning Mom's funeral until after she passed away. Mom had left a directive to be cremated, and prepaid arrangements had been made at the time of Dad's death, so there was not much to do except contact the National Cemetery in Dallas and select a date.

Susan was the first to broach the subject. She wanted the service scheduled for the following summer after she and her husband returned from their sail trip. They had already experienced other delays and the seasonal timeframe was narrowing for them to sail around South Africa. In addition, she wanted her husband to be able to attend the service.

We understood her position and came to easy agreement to delay mom's funeral until next summer.

• • •

The extreme heat continued through August and blew into September as high winds and parched lands sparked massive fires throughout Central Texas. It was heartbreaking to witness such destruction and loss. Daily commuting and work routines proceeded in somewhat a surreal state as the fires and tragedies continued throughout the remaining summer, generating senses of uncertainty, but also of community and giving.

The ACL Festival weekend offered a much-welcomed escape from the fires, my increasing facial pain and thoughts of the impending joint replacement surgery. Trey and I marked the line-up schedule with acts we wanted to catch over the three-day festival. This festival would be the first in eight years in which no impending or potential parent related crisis overshadowed the excitement. I intended to enjoy the weekend and music to the fullest extent, and did so.

I looked forward most to seeing Coldplay. Trey and I headed to the AMD stage, located on the west side of Zilker Park, a good hour before the band's show. The weekend had started with a break from the heat, which had the happy effect of increasing the friendliness of festival goers, and adding to the senses of excitement and magic as the sun set over West Austin. We settled our blanket on a spot just left of center stage and about 150 feet out.

Chris Martin and his band did not disappoint. The show was an amazing experience. Laser lights danced wildly as the crowd sang along to familiar lyrics. One particular song started out slow with Mr. Martin seated at his upright painted piano. I listened carefully, trying to identify the song while the intro extended longer than usual.

Mr. Martin sang in a soft, light tone,

> *When you try your best, but you don't succeed;*
>
> *When you get what you want, but not what you need;*
>
> *When you feel so tired, but you can't sleep...*

It was not a song I had heard before. I stood still – struck by the lyrics that seemed to be talking to me, about how I truly felt.

> *Stuck in reverse;*
>
> *And the tears come streaming down your face;*
>
> *When you lose something you can't replace;*
>
> *When you love someone, but it goes to waste;*
>
> *Could it be worse?*

As the tempo increased and built up to the last chorus, tears streamed down my face. To my immediate right stood a middle-aged, brunette woman in jeans and a long-sleeved blouse. She had not been there before, but now her face perched just off my right shoulder staring at me. Since she seemed concerned I guessed that she had spotted the fresh scar running down the right side of my face and neck. I acknowledged her, but was more focused on the musical magic. As always, my brain searched for something or someone in my life to attach the song and surreal moment to. Trey had stepped forward out of arm's reach and several people separated us. He was in his own world. *No, this is my experience, and these are my problems.*

As Mr. Martin ended with,

> *Lights will guide you home;*
>
> *And ignite your bones;*
>
> *And I will try and fix you.*

a strong sense of gratitude fell over me like light, and my brain connected the song and moment to Dr. Kaye—the guy who had "accepted" me and would fix my jaw.

The strangely overdressed woman's face still lingered at my shoulder, invading my emotional space. I later wondered if she was aware of what she had witnessed.

Had she known what was going on in my head? Had she seen the seed of gratitude implanting into my subconscious?

Chapter 9
WE ARE GOING TO HELP YOU

I hadn't always trusted my inner voice. I'm not one to say where the sense of deep knowing comes from and I had only generally abided by it. Like when my inner voice told me my dad needed a hot breakfast the morning he died. However, the strong senses that came over me while soaking in my bathtub soon after ACL were different. I didn't know what they related to, just that I would be facing a difficult challenge aside from the jaw joint replacement, while these words rose into my head...

"We are going to help you."

I didn't really think too much about the experience. I just accepted it and carried on with my life. During times of quiet, usually while winding down in the bathtub, I would sort of "check in" with myself. The strong senses were still there... difficult challenge, not the surgery, and I would not be alone.

PART THREE

NOT ACCEPTING OR TRUSTING

Our struggles are opportunities for
growth and to realign with our
true selves and what we love

Accept whatever comes your way
and *Trust* that the Universe
is ultimately on your side

Chapter 10
A VEIL OF DARKNESS

Hours previously devoted to my mother were filled with overseeing the various estate closure processes and making up for lost time at work. I carried on as if I weren't exhausted. I was also unaware of all the unprocessed emotions and grief I carried. *Forward Progress Always!*

My office had been instructed to conduct a research study over the interim period before the next legislative session. One of the study's two subjects was in my area of expertise, so I was a tad disappointed to return to work following the June surgery to learn that a researcher/writer had been contracted to perform the work. However, with another surgery impending I was in no position to protest and had come to accept it as a necessary blessing when Mom entered the active dying state. I was glad to help the contracted writer and shared my years of accumulated research, data, spreadsheets, and knowledge. I remained an active contributing member of the study team, and that was more than enough for me and my ego at the time.

Progress on the house renovation halted soon after it began. Since that time, both daughters had purchased their own homes and my mother passed away. With each move, furniture and sentimental keepsakes got left behind due to some reason or another.

A decade earlier, this practice had been established when we moved Trey's father to Austin from Richmond, Virginia. In all, and over the course of the decade, Trey and I moved our daughters back and forth between schools a total of eight times, we helped them move in and around Austin six times, we relocated Trey's father three times, and we moved one or both of my parents six times. Lacking the time to deal with everybody's residual "stuff," our house in effect became a storage facility. Like the burdens of caring for my ailing parents, this stuff was not solely ours to carry, yet we were.

Our double garage was impassable as was Meredith's bedroom, where furniture was crammed from wall-to-wall and boxes stacked to the ceiling. Lindsey's bedroom looked just as it did the day she left for college except something occupied every available space under the bed, in drawers, and in the closet, as did every cabinet and closet space throughout the rest of our house.

We kept the chaos out of sight so we could host friends from time to time. Anyone who looked behind the wrong door would have surmised we were hoarders. The correct assessment, however, was that the order and peace we projected were merely façades. Although Trey and I had not chosen to live with the closed off and carefully avoided messy spaces that had accumulated over time, that was our reality – an external existence with an uncanny resemblance to our internal lives.

• • •

While waiting for Dr. Kaye to arrive for the pre-operative appointment, Trey and I chatted with another resident surgeon, one more relaxed and confident. The discussion had moved onto music by the time Dr. Kaye entered the examining room. We exchanged hellos and Trey asked if his son liked the University of Texas. A broad, proud smile came over Dr. Kaye's face. "Yes, he's very much enjoying it! My wife just left for Austin to visit."

The exam was routine except for the pain in my right TMJ joint, which had greatly increased, making it difficult to handle the pressure Dr. Kaye applied. He again explained what the surgery would entail – a small surgical saw would be used to remove the condylar and coronoid processes and the custom fitted prostheses would be inserted and secured with screws. The surgery was expected to take about two hours, and I would require six to eight weeks of healing before resuming yoga, running, and other physical activities. This was consistent with what I had read online.

He reminded me that my mouth would be wired shut when I woke, and added that he would also have to wake me before inserting the wires in order to test my facial nerves. He ran his finger over the three-month old scar, motioned the resident surgeon over, and pressing into my neck, said, "See, we're going to use this same line as the incision."

I had previously been told that the surgery would require a two-night stay in the hospital, but learned at this appointment that Dr. Kaye intended to release me after one night if I were well enough. Trey would be required to remove a tube delivering anesthesia to the area of the cut bone. Our eyes met and we both squirmed.

I spoke up. "I'm not comfortable—"

"Oh, it will be fine," Dr. Kaye said. "You can do it."

I was not so sure. I just wanted to get the surgery over with as soon as possible. Perhaps I projected an attitude of treating the surgery lightly and Dr. Kaye's statement, "We are going to assault you!" was an attempt to get my attention.

The picture that came to mind was one of being hit upside the head with a baseball bat. I was ready to leave. The resident surgeon noticed the change in my disposition as he stood with me explaining paperwork. When I signed the last form and followed Trey toward the door, he called out, "Don't worry, you're in good hands."

I passed over the threshold and followed Trey to the right. Rounding the corner, I caught a glimpse of Dr. Kaye standing nearby. "Yes, that's one thing I am grateful for," I said.

• • •

I had been firm in asking—just shy of demanding—that our daughters be present for my surgery. One, I hadn't seen them much. They were both new to their careers, and I missed having at least one of them living at home and being part of my daily life. Two, I did not have confidence in Trey's ability to care for me following the surgery, and he didn't seem to have confidence in himself. Several times he had expressed apprehensions about going it alone.

At the hospital's surgery center, the check-in clerk informed us that my surgery was "level one." She didn't explain what that meant except mine was first on the schedule. Later I discovered it also meant I was assigned to the first pre-operative room, which was spacious enough to hold Trey and both the girls.

Right away, I inspected the hospital gown's slits over both breasts and was glad to find them taut and nip-slip proof. Also to my relief, the anesthesiologist was not the same one I had flashed in June.

The assisting surgeon showed up next and introduced himself as Dr. Davis. He was professional, yet personable, pleasant, and reassuring. Before leaving, he labeled my right jaw joint with a marker. Last to arrive was Dr. Kaye. He shook Trey's hand, and I introduced our daughters. He stood at the foot of my bed and discussed expectations and offered answers to last minute questions. Upbeat, he shared his reassurance by grabbing and shaking my toes through the blanket, and then turned to face the wall to my right and used it to prop up a clipboard as he jotted notes.

Trey inquired about what I would be allowed to drink through the tiny stir-stick straw, which is what I would be limited to immediately after the surgery. Dr. Kaye kept his back to my family as he turned his gaze from the clipboard to me and, making light of the question, responded in a suggestive tone, "A beer?"

My face flushed rendering me unable to meet his eyes, but I saw he anticipated my response. I flashed an awkward thumbs-up sign and smirked into space.

As I was being wheeled into the operating room, a tinge of panic rose in my chest as all moisture disappeared from my oral cavity. I asked the nurses pushing me into surgery if they had caused it.

"Yep!"

"My mouth feels as dry as Texas!"

That made them laugh, but I wasn't trying to be funny. Breathing had become unpleasant. The other pre-operative drugs began taking effect as I moved onto the narrow operating table and watched my gown fall from my shoulders after one of the nurses tugged its strings.

What is she…?

• • •

"Martha, Martha!"

I struggled to open my eyes and through heavy lids I saw Dr. Kaye's face, it seemed to be floating directly in front of mine. "Martha."

I strained to focus but my eyes didn't cooperate and I heard him again, "Martha, look at me…"

• • •

No peaceful, colorful dream surfaced as I gained consciousness in the recovery room, perhaps due to the substitution of Dilaudid for morphine given my previous experience with nausea. Bright lights stung through my eyelids and my neck hurt from being propped forward with a pillow. I solved both problems by pulling the pillow out from under my head and placing it over my face.

My tongue burned and seemed to be stuck to the left side of my teeth. The memory of my parched mouth caused me to rationalize that my tongue must be stuck to my teeth, like it had touched a frozen metal pole. That was my drug-induced reasoning. All I knew was that my tongue seared and

I couldn't move it.

The nurses and I competed on the pillow's placement – it alternated between over my face and under my head several times before a nurse realized that the lights were bothering me and replaced the pillow with a small towel for my eyes. I tried to explain that my tongue was stuck, but they either didn't understand me through clinched teeth and wires, or disregarded my utterances as post-anesthesia babble.

My neck bled where the anesthetic tube was inserted. The nurses cleaned and taped the area a couple of times before the bleeding abated enough to move me into a regular room. As I was rolled into what should have been a healing bastion, I looked forward to seeing my family's faces. But my room was vacant and I passed back out. Once again, some administrative anomaly occurred and kept Trey and the girls from receiving word that I had been moved from recovery.

By early evening, I could stay awake for a reasonable amount of time. My tongue was still stuck despite my earlier efforts to moisten the area, and I realized that it was throbbing and couldn't be freed because my teeth had been closed over it and wired shut.

Trey ordered some vegetable broth and helped me while I sipped it through a stir-stick straw. He voiced his frustration while reciting the exchanges between him and the waiting room clerk. He was exasperated, and I wasn't up to hearing about it. A headache had developed in and around my forehead while my smashed tongue pulsated between my upper and lower molars. I needed and wanted to have my family with me for support; I didn't have the energy to absorb his irritation or offer sympathy.

Both Drs. Kaye and Davis visited in the early evening along with a third physician, Dr. Augustine, who seemed annoyed, as if the other two had been teasing him. As Dr. Kaye checked the taped area on my neck, I tried to relay my tongue's predicament. He couldn't understand me and became impatient. "You're just going… mhwaa, mhwaa, mhwaa," mimicking me.

I was stunned. *That's because my freaking tongue is stuck between my teeth!*

But I was in a hospital bed, and my parents taught me to obey authority, and this guy still had to remove my stitches, and unwire my mouth, and I would be seeing him for at least another three years. So, I stopped trying to talk and sat still through his examination like an admonished child.

As the three doctors stood at the foot of my bed ready to leave, I had an opportunity to weigh in. I was clear and delicate about the situation, yet none of them seemed to believe me. With my mangled, half-operational tongue I persisted until Dr. Kaye turned to the still-annoyed Dr. Augustine and said, "Check on it tonight."

I sensed the directive was made only to appease me, but the success motivated me to press on. "Thiz wap awound my head is too tight, itz cauzin a headache." As I said this, and without thinking, my hand rose to loosen the wrap, which sent Trey and the girls lunging toward me with outreached arms. "Nooo!"

Dr. Kaye waved them off. "It's okay. She won't fall apart." He always seemed to perceive me as stronger than I actually was, probably because that is the persona I projected. That's how I wanted people to see me, but the truth was that I would most certainly fall apart.

Dr. Davis asked, "Do you drink coffee? Sometimes the lack of caffeine can cause headaches."

I replied, "I do dwink coffee," and nodded as if I had just been enlightened. I did drink coffee, but only half-caffeinated and generally only one cup a day, and never after noon. Caffeine withdrawal was not the issue but I opted to play stupid rather than challenge Dr. Davis' assertion.

Dr. Kaye loosened the wrap around my head anyway. Within minutes, the headache was gone. My tongue still throbbed though.

Sometime in the evening, after Trey and Lindsey left for the hotel, a frustrated Dr. Augustine showed up again. "Are you sure your tongue is caught? It's going to require that I cut one of the primary fixation wires. Are you sure you want me to do that?"

"Yeth, I'm thure."

"What side did you say it was?"

"Left."

He first attempted to use the wire cutters tied to my gown. I was told they would be there following the surgery, but hadn't yet noticed them. They were to be carried on myself as an extra appendage in the event of an emergency situation, such as a claustrophobia-induced panic attack or to prevent choking while vomiting. Luckily, nausea hadn't been a problem because the thought of throwing up was terrifying.

The wire cutters were not sharp enough, so Dr. Augustine resorted to finding another pair that were also not ideal based on the effort and time he spent cutting the main left wire. Through sheer determination, I dislodged my battered tongue without having to have the right fixation wire cut.

Before Dr. Augustine began rewiring, I mentioned new pain that had developed under the right side of my tongue. "I'm curious to know if it's been cut, that's what it feels like."

"Do you want me to cut the right fixation wire?" His voice sounded a bit threatening – not menacing, but rather manipulative, like when a parent offers their child an absurd alternative intended solely to coerce the child the parent's way. I declined.

Meredith volunteered to take the night shift and helped me through the evening as necessary. This was very generous as her 5'10" frame didn't fit comfortably on the "guest bed" that also served as a window seat. As we turned in for the evening, she retrieved my phone and launched the

"Healing" playlist I had created especially for the hospital stay. As Enya and Celtic magic serenaded us to sleep, my mind and body sought to regain a sense of security.

The hours passed with just one assisted trip to the bathroom, and the nurses were quiet during their regular checks. The checks sometimes included an abdominal injection of some anti-clotting medication, a standard practice following surgeries at DFW Metro – I was not special. At least I anticipated them – the two shots back in June had been another surprise, a particularly harsh one. During this hospital stay, I lost count of the injections and failed to note the number of bruises on my stomach.

In a daze, I woke before dawn to find a physician standing over me with a small flashlight and trying to insert a tongue depressor between my lips. He uttered something as I struggled to wake, and I then realized who he was and what he was doing. Proud of my lucidity, I pointed at him and declared, "Dr. Augustine."

An actual smile. "Yes."

I positioned my head to make it easier for him to see the area he had re-wired hours earlier. Shining light onto my assemblage of teeth, brackets and wires, he asked, "Has Dr. Kaye been by this morning?"

"No."

There were no adjustments and with a click of the flashlight, he turned and left.

Mid-morning, Dr. Kaye arrived and gave my toes another friendly shake. "Hello! You're looking good. Have you been to the bathroom yet?"

"Yes."

"Good. It's time to remove the wrapping around your head."

Feeling stronger and perhaps a little less vulnerable, my true self announced, "My headache disappeared right after you loosened this last night."

Dr. Kaye acknowledged my point with a cordial apology and proceeded to unpack the cotton gauze in my ear canal. Using an otoscope, he checked on stitches inside my canal then inserted a long Q-tip type stick to remove a blood clot. "There, that should feel better."

My ear did feel relief, but from pressure I had hardly noticed and assumed was normal. However, the left side of my tongue was still raw and aching, as was the area under the right side of my tongue. I said nothing about those areas.

Dr. Kaye approved my discharge for later in the afternoon, contingent upon my continued progress. I was to contact his office to schedule a one-week post-operative appointment, not lift anything over ten pounds, and hold off on physical activities for six to eight weeks. Together, the two incisions extended farther down my neck and higher above my ear than the one had in June. Treatment was the same though – leave them uncovered and regularly apply antibacterial ointment.

Before departing, Dr. Kaye made sure I understood how and when to remove the tubing from my neck. As an afterthought, he informed me that a black rubber cap should be attached to the end of the tube. "You need to make sure that cap comes out with the tube."

An image came to mind of a dislodged rubber cap stuck inside my neck. I eyed Dr. Kaye waiting for him to address the obvious question. He was teasing me with his silence, eyeballing right back and forcing me to ask, "And if it doesn't come out?"

His eyes warmed and a grin spread over his face as he pointed at me and laughed, "Call me."

My eyes fixed on his and I felt warmth in his smile. Although not reassured, I returned the smile as he backed out the door. This news left me even more apprehensive about Trey being the one to remove the tubing. I also didn't feel anywhere near ready to leave the hospital.

After noon, I ventured to the bathroom alone and caught myself in the mirror. No one had warned I wouldn't recognize myself. The first comparison that came to mind was the Sloth character from *The Goonies* movie. That was an exaggeration, but also the closest resemblance to the reflection staring back at me. My face had been assaulted: the entire right side was swollen, particularly the area along my jawline, which was as big as a baseball; the hair above my ear had been shaved where the incision extended onto my scalp; and my right eyebrow sagged where I had sustained nerve damage. It turned out that I also had nerve damage below the right corner of my mouth, but that wasn't evident at the time due to swelling.

My readiness to leave changed with the clock and as my strength returned. The Dilaudid was stopped in the early afternoon with no repercussions, and the hospital cafeteria staff kindly indulged my regular requests for apple juice and vegetable broth.

By mid-afternoon, the girls had left for Austin and I was on my laptop answering work emails and coordinating speakers for a public forum to kick off the research study. Before taking off for surgery, all speakers had been confirmed and I had submitted a draft agenda with general topics of discussion. But a lot of details were left pending.

I had received emails from two of the guest speakers who wanted to talk about specific content. I was hoping to avoid informing them of my surgery, but the two phone call requests forced me to divulge my current condition. I told the former state representative that my boss would give her a call as soon as possible. The other speaker, a colleague working at another state agency, graciously accepted my plea for a one-week reprieve.

• • •

The clock neared 6:00 p.m. when the attendant wheeled me to the patient pick-up area where Trey and I waited for his car. I enjoyed being outside, but avoided looking at others arriving and departing around the hospital's circle drive. Since catching the concerned looks of nurses while passing their station, I had kept my head tilted down and inward in an attempt to hide the right side of my face.

This vanity was forgotten at the sight of Trey's small white Volvo coming up and around the drive. Trey and I heard his car before seeing it, and dismay took over as we realized the noise came from a headlight dragging across the pavement alongside his car. The front right side of his car had been smashed and the headlight dangled from its wiring underneath the front bumper. The valet runner pulled up to the curb and stepped out to convey the car over to Trey as if all was normal.

Trey pointed to the headlight. "Uh-mmm, that is not how I left my car."

The valet acted as if he had just noticed the headlight. "It wasn't like that when you got here?"

"No. Uh-mmm, I need to see a supervisor."

I really should have given Trey more credit at the time for managing his anger. Particularly considering he had to have his car's wheels realigned after my June hospital stay, the last time it was valet-parked at DFW Metro Hospital.

• • •

Trey helped me into the hotel room's bed and left to fill three prescriptions – liquid pain killer, liquid antibiotic, and antiseptic mouthwash.

The following afternoon, I took my first shower, which offered the best location to attempt the removal of the tubing in the event of leaking or bleeding. The two of us were equally tense. Because I felt faint, I ended up sitting down on the edge of the tub on Trey's second attempt. We were both relieved to see the black plastic cap still clinging to the end of the tube.

I consumed liquids pretty much constantly, but they were hardly enough to satisfy my metabolism. My stomach always felt empty since what was going in came out at the same pace and consistency. I was ready to get home to Austin, and take over the responsibility of feeding myself. When it came time to pack and check out of the hotel, this strong desire fueled my strength. It also had me squelching feelings of anxiety that arose while packing – I was afraid of Interstate 35 and Trey's driving, and I was unsure of his Volvo with its headlight duct-taped inside its bumper.

After packing, I sat down on the girls' unmade sleeper sofa and finished a bottle of Green Machine Naked Juice. Trey was also packed and gathering a load of bags to take to the car just as a wave of nausea hit. The liquefied green fruits and vegetables were not mixing well with my stomach's unexpressed anxiety. I tried to speak to get Trey's attention but only managed a long groan which, combined with my flailing hands, communicated my panicked state. Unsure of what was happening, he lunged toward me and tripped over the stacked luggage. By the time he made it to my side, I was heaving uncontrollably as my stomach rejected the green juice and forced it into my mouth.

I used my breath to spray the juice out between my wired teeth and onto the white sheets. As my stomached emptied, I focused on keeping the rhythm of my breath in sync with the heaves and was able to avoid choking. Several minutes passed before I stopped shaking, and a good hour passed before I was ready to venture out and onto Interstate 35.

• • •

I had no clue as to the extent my body had been traumatized. A recliner in our family room provided the optimal sleeping experience for me, while invading Trey's space and television time. This arrangement should have prompted compromises between our internal time zone differences. But posturing Trey into a compromise had never been a light and nimble endeavor, and I was the queen of compromises, always putting my family's wants and needs above my own. So I never pushed for peace and quiet… I failed to respect my own exhaustion… *forward progress always!*

On the second evening home and as the T.V. blared, an overwhelming urge to exercise came over me; like I had to train to get in shape for something. I escaped into the quiet darkness of my bedroom, mounted Trey's stationary bicycle, and peddled at a pace strong enough to break a sweat. Mesmerized at the minutes accumulating on the bicycle's digital timer, I clinched the handlebar and peddled through the shadows.

After five minutes or so, I sensed an obscure presence in front of me. I looked up from the timer but couldn't see what I felt – a manifestation, like a floating veil of darkness suspended before me just beyond reach. I kept peddling. I wasn't afraid, even as an engulfing sadness forced tears from a depth of my being I had not known existed. Keeping a steady pace, I sobbed for another ten minutes.

The rational part of my brain decided, *This must be what it feels like to be depressed.*

The dark veil disappeared, yet I cried off and on for the next two days, unable to identify any particular reason, emotion, or situation to explain it. During this time, I awoke to something poking the left corner of my lips. Using my fingers, I found a hardened scab-like area and pulled on it, thinking it was dry skin.

What detached from my lip was a small piece of plastic line – a tied stitch. The left corner of my mouth had been cut and sewn up and I had just found out about it.

Chapter 11
YOU CAN RETURN
TO NORMAL ACTIVITY

The unexplained tears subsided as did whatever emotional, psychological, or spiritual darkness that seemed to have possessed me. I was not depressed. The darkness was more like a lingering memory, a compartmentalized heaviness within my body, small enough to ignore.

Strength was slow to recover and difficult to maintain on a smoothie diet. It made no sense that the timeframe for returning to work following the parotidectomy was two weeks, while the time indicated by Dr. Kaye for the jaw reconstruction was only a week. I didn't question Dr. Kaye about this, instead I self-prescribed two weeks off, even though I felt like I needed a month. The predominant reason to delay my return was how the liquid diet affected my digestive system. I needed quick and constant access to a bathroom and was not willing to deal with such unpleasantness at work.

• • •

Ten days after the surgery, Trey semi-carefully navigated the madness of Interstate 35 to deliver me to what would be my first of seven post-operative appointments. Although the examinations were all routine, each appointment introduced new and increasing curiosities, strangeness, levels of unease, and unasked and unanswered questions.

With this first appointment, my face was still very swollen and I was uncomfortable with my appearance, but the first order of business was cutting the fixation wires and opening my mouth wide enough to brush my teeth. A frightening, but manageable, endeavor. I was only able to open my mouth wide enough to fit the toothbrush in, so the brushing job was mediocre at best. Dr. Kaye checked my bite alignment, mouth-opening ability, and facial nerves. "You should regain the ability to raise your eyebrow in about four weeks."

The next step was to remove the sutures. They were very different from those Dr. Abbey had made in June, which lay on top of the skin like crossties on a train track. These lay underneath the skin and seemed to intertwine the entire lengths of the healing incisions. Removal was a matter of finding the small knots, cutting them, and then pulling on the long strands until they cleared the skin.

Excitement and vigor seemed to emanate from Dr. Kaye causing him to rush through the process, so I concentrated on being still. He then explained what the one-month follow-up appointment would entail: removal of the arch bar, which he preferred to keep in place until proper alignment of my bite could be confirmed; and the start of physical therapy if my mouth opening had not drastically improved. And he again relayed the timelines for resuming physical activities and three years of follow-up appointments.

The best news was that my sustenance no longer had to come from a blender. I had lost seven pounds since leaving the hospital, which traumatized my body further through what felt like starvation. I was weak, and some internal voice, that I failed to appease, screamed incessantly for nourishment. I could begin with soft foods, and Dr. Kaye began listing naturally soft foods. All I heard were "eggs" and "pancakes."

As the appointment ended, Dr. Kaye perched on a little rolling stool to the left of the dental examining chair where I sat. Trey occupied a chair in front of me. Everything that needed to be covered had been, and I had no further questions. We reached the point where a physician would step into their natural position of authority to verbally and nonverbally acknowledge the obvious conclusion of the need for further engagement, essentially granting permission to those present to leave.

That time came and went and an awkward silence took over the room.

I remained facing forward but not really looking at anything. In the periphery, I could see Dr. Kaye was staring at me with a troubled expression. After a few moments, I grew more self-conscious – I hated the way I looked and was worried about the rate of healing.

Yet, instead of turning to him and saying, *Is there ever going to be a point when I will recognize myself?* I sat there in silence, believing he was horrified by the way I looked and that he was afraid he had botched the surgery.

After about twenty seconds—an excruciatingly long period of time to exist in awkwardness—Dr. Kaye reclaimed his role and broke the silence. We were glad to be released. I rose from the dental chair with the lingering thought that Dr. Kaye felt responsible for how awful I looked. In some weird effort to ease his state of distress, I turned and faced him before exiting the examining room, leaned in, and whispered, "Thank you."

Dr. Kaye's eyebrows rose and his eyes popped open. I didn't really think about his reaction except perhaps that it was over the top. As Trey and I entered the hallway, my attention moved onto a more pressing subject, "I want scrambled eggs and blueberry pancakes."

Heading toward a nearby breakfast diner, I pulled down the passenger seat's visor mirror to check out my mouth. I gasped! The top of my tongue had turned black and grayish-blue stains covered my teeth.

"There's algae growing in my mouth!"

"What?"

"Look!"

"I don't think that's algae."

"What is this?" Using my fingernails, I scoured my tongue and teeth. "It's not coming off!"

Trey tried to calm me and insisted I call Dr. Kaye's nurse. Before agreeing, I pulled the bottle of prescribed antiseptic mouthwash from my bag and read the entire wordy label for the first time. Printed near the bottom was the statement, "May temporarily stain teeth."

Someone should have pointed out this important information. It was my fault for not reading all the fine print, but who does that? It was mouthwash! I had exceeded the recommended usage because it soothed the areas where my tongue had been cut. Now the evidence of that overuse covered my tongue and teeth – the perfect complements to my swollen face and droopy eyebrow.

My belief that Dr. Kaye had rushed through the sutures' removal was confirmed the following weekend. I noticed two areas—one near the top of my ear and another just below it—that felt unusually hard; too hard to be scabs. By angling my face between a handheld mirror and wall mirror, I got a clear view to check them out.

Dr. Kaye had missed removing one of the long stitches intertwined through my ear and neck. A phone call the following Monday relieved my fear of having to drive up Interstate 35. The plastic line would eventually dissolve on its own, and I could cut off the ends, which had since become unknotted and were dangling about a quarter inch out of my skin.

• • •

A seed of gratitude had been planted four weeks prior to that first post-operative appointment. I was not aware of exactly when that seed sprouted roots, but it had done so without my permission. I first noticed the emergence of its stems in the form of thoughts during the week leading up to the second post-op appointment – thoughts like weeds, prickly, but with a bloom of cotton-like softness. I questioned how and why they sprang up and snipped them in the bud. Because at the time I didn't recognize what they were, I didn't think to journey deep to address the roots. So, like weeds, the thoughts popped back up after pruning.

• • •

The longing to hit the open road alone had persisted since Trey's and my initial drive to DFW six months earlier. I desired time alone. I wanted to drive myself and reclaim some sense of control. I wanted to listen to my music and through it, find myself and be myself again, even if it was only for a day.

I was also ready to have Trey stop escorting me into doctor appointments. Always seeking a sense of control, he would interrupt and correct me. Although not his intent, Trey's presence was as much patronizing as it was supportive.

As the one-month, post-operative appointment approached, I was again faced with the circumstance of trying to balance my needs with Trey's feelings – a reoccurring theme in our lives together. My true-self is fiercely independent; however, my medical needs and my mother's death had forced dependence on Trey, and I again slipped into accommodation mode. A default co-dependent existence that Trey preferred. For me, the underlying environment still consisted of messy areas we chose not to visit – just like the closed-off spaces in our home hiding accumulated stuff that we lacked the time and will to tackle.

I made a weak attempt at suggesting I drive alone, although I presented it solely as a concern about Trey missing too much work. Not completely a lie, but I felt guilty enough to give in at his first protest. The guilt wasn't only tied to being misleading, but it also resulted from a curiosity that had developed within me—the desire to test my blossoming thoughts and feelings.

Trey and I left work at noon for the 4:00 p.m. appointment. I again sat in the passenger seat of his white Volvo in silent disappointment. When Trey was around, I was not fully me; I was not the strong, intelligent, independent person I was at work and with friends. That is the individual I wanted Dr. Kaye to see.

What the fuck? Why do I care how Dr. Kaye sees me? Snip!

• • •

The procedure took place in a stark oversized room rather than a regular examining room. The single dental chair at its center appeared small and ominous. It was hard to imagine that the room's grey walls and empty spaces had ever provided comfort to those with a misfortunate need to be there.

The nurse was prepping a syringe to numb my gums before removal of the arch bar secured to the front of my teeth. The bar was held in place by thin wires laced through my gums in between each tooth, and I was eager to have all of it out. I resolved to forgo the Novocain shots. The fear of more needles, particularly in my mouth, outweighed any fear of pain from having wires pulled out of my gums.

I could handle pain. I was a master of pain.

Trey faced me as he leaned against a wall a good fifteen feet away from where I sat in the dental chair. Since we were both tired and had covered the usual surface level topics on the drive, we waited for Dr. Kaye in silence. After about ten minutes, a physician stepped into the open doorway and gave us a curious glance while surveying the rest of the room.

I waved in an effort to acknowledge our existences, and he reluctantly nodded before turning to leave. Smiles spread in unison across our faces as I leaned toward Trey and whispered, "It's the man at the top of the stairs!"

Dr. Kaye's office was located on the second floor of Office Building One, a name very much reflective of the building's lack of ambiance. The first floor consisted of a large open atrium half filled with small two-seat tables, and a tiny snack bar tucked under a wide, open stairway leading to a second floor landing. By now, Trey and I had trekked up that stairway eight times. On many previous visits, we had observed that doctor hanging out at the top of the stairs and talking on his cell phone. Hence, his man-of-mystery nickname, "the man at the top of the stairs."

Thanks to an effective topical solution, the removal of the wires was tolerable. Dr. Kaye seemed anxious, or maybe he was just in a hurry again. I remained calm and unmoving while he clipped all the wires. His cutters were much sharper than Dr. Augustine's.

Using plyers, he'd grip a frayed wire and yank back clearing the long strands in one motion. After the first couple of wires, he said, "Wow, I'm impressed! You had no Novocain, right?"

Rather than divulge my greater fear of needles, I responded, "No, I'm okay though."

In his anxiousness or haste, he missed cutting a wire and when he tried pulling it out, my head jerked up a good foot. The assistant had to point out where the wire needed to be cut. It was all over in about ten minutes, and Dr. Kaye disappeared from the office as I gathered my belongings to leave.

He returned with a rehab "device" that was really just a handful of tongue depressors stacked and held together at both ends with medical tape. My physical therapy three times a day was to wrench my mouth open wide enough to insert the stack and leave it there 30 seconds, working my way up to a minute. Once I mastered longer times without pain, I was to add a depressor, slowly and torturously stretching my jaw muscles and teaching them to work again.

Before leaving, Dr. Kaye made me demonstrate that I could do it for fifteen seconds. I couldn't open wide enough at first, but used my fingers to pry my teeth apart just enough to wedge the bundle of sticks a fraction beyond the edges of my bottom and top front teeth. Dr. Kaye smiled in delight.

Is he some kind of sadist?

The pain was excruciating. I held onto the dental chair for support, then sat down when I became faint. Once settled, I assured myself, *Okay, I can do this.*

Turning away from Dr. Kaye's glee, I focused on the slow moving second hand of a nearby wall clock, counting each passing second while I concentrated on keeping tears from welling up. I made it through the fifteen seconds and then expressed my bewilderment as to why a local anesthetic had been recommended for the earlier procedure when this, by far, was more agonizing.

With Trey at my side, a plastic bag of tongue depressors in hand, and with relief, I left. My recent thoughts were not supported by seeing Dr. Kaye. Seeing him standing there in his oversized physician's coat with a funny smile, I assured myself, *No, I'm not attracted to him.*

• • •

Even though it was painful, particularly in the first few weeks, I was diligent with the physical therapy. It was also effective. I added a depressor a week, and progressed to two a week until I reached a total of twenty tongue depressors, or forty millimeters, which is within the jaw's normal range of motion. I also followed directives related to returning to my usual physical activities.

I really missed yoga. As I breathed into my first downward-facing dog and stretched my arms, straightening my spine and opening my hips, emotions stirred and were released. I couldn't hold back tears as my body forced some recognition of the battering it had endured, I told my classmates I was just really happy to be back.

Another week passed before I attempted running. Beginning in 1991, Austin's staple sub shop has sponsored a five-mile "Turkey Trot" each Thanksgiving morning. The race wends through downtown Austin and had been a family tradition since 1997. My face was still swollen, but strength had returned enough that I was determined to participate with my family and 15,000 other runners.

It was a beautiful fall morning – not untypical for Austin; sunny yet cool, crisp air, and an endless blue sky. I didn't run. Barely lifting my running shoes off the pavement at a pace slow enough to sustain the full five-miles, what I did was closer to an actual trot. The downhill portions proved to be too much pressure on my new jaw joint, so Trey and I walked those. He stayed by my side through the entire race and we talked and admired the people, costumes, and scenes along the route. It was Austin at its best weird.

Our relationship had improved but we were still avoiding the honest conversations necessary to unleash and resolve, or not resolve, my old resentments. It was easier for both of us to just not go there – simply to keep those doors shut.

By Christmas, I was feeling much better than what my "feeling good" had been before the surgeries. The use of my right eyebrow had returned, but the swelling in my face had lessened enough to expose the nerve damage around and below my lower right lip. My smile was crooked and I had trouble fully pronouncing words that required use of muscles in that area. Many of those words I had to use in my job, such as actuarial, calculated, and probably.

• • •

The three-month post-operative appointment was scheduled for mid-January. Logistics conveniently had me flying alone to the appointment as I had continued to long for a sense of independence and control. I also remained curious about my still sprouting thoughts and feelings, but certainly had no intention of discussing them with Dr. Kaye.

A good thirty minutes before my scheduled appointment, I arrived at Office Building One and found a table in the café area tucked under the stairway. I felt anxious for some reason, so I pulled out an unfinished Sudoku puzzle from the *Austin American-Statesman* to provide focus and occupy the time. I also worked on finishing a bottle of water, and glanced up from the puzzle to take a sip just in time to catch a glimpse of Dr. Kaye rounding the corner and entering a door.

My heart spring boarded from my chest! He hadn't seen me, yet my throat was tightening, my heart pounding, and I was close to hyperventilating. I didn't understand why my body reacted in such a way. *This isn't me, I need to gain control.*

By the time I settled into an examining room, I managed to steady my breathing and regain a relaxed appearance. My blood pressure failed to maintain the ruse though, and the nurse flashed a concerned look my way.

With a sheepish grin, I proposed, "White-coat syndrome?"

I didn't understand why I was so anxious and tried to calm myself once alone and waiting for Dr. Kaye. Unfortunately, the wait wasn't long enough, so I compensated by talking as little as possible.

Taking the lead after the obligatory hellos, Dr. Kaye became tongue-tied while attempting informal chit-chat. It was awkward and we were both glad to move onto the regular routine of the post-operative examination. My bite was still aligned, mouth opening was within normal range, and another set of panoramic x-rays revealed that all screws were properly secured, while areas on the right side of my face were either numb, tingling, or painful to touch. Dr. Kaye rubbed his finger along the length of the scar on my neck. "This is healing nicely, but I can refer you to a plastic surgeon if you're interested."

More anesthetic and knives? "No thanks, I'm fine."

Despite having several questions, I didn't ask them. My slow rate of healing bothered me. I was worried about my crooked smile, damaged nerves, and still swollen jaw line, but remained silent and ready to get the heck out of there.

As the appointment wound down, Dr. Kaye sat at my feet on his little rolling stool and went over the timeline for the remaining follow-up visits – at this point I could have recited it backwards but remained mute as he droned on. His routine speech ended with, "…sometime around April 19th… I will see you again in April, when it's… Hot!"

"Hot" was strangely emphasized. Not louder, just with inflection – the "h" was more of an "hh," the "o" an "oo," and the "t" was accentuated with a small jerk of his head which had the effect of an exclamation point.

Picturesque fields of bluebonnets appeared in my mind… *Hot in April? April is gorgeous – it's not hot in April, there are bluebonnets!*

Together, we stood to leave and our eyes met. The color drained from his face and with somber intention he said, "You can return to normal activity."

After the micro-second it took my brain to process his statement, I thought, *He means sex!*

I darted past him to retrieve my purse. Even though that timeframe had been discussed ad nauseam and had long since passed, rationale weighed in. *Normal activities? Okay, there's yoga, the turkey trot, and I skied for five days.*

With my back to him, I responded with a dismissive, "Oh, I have," and rummaged through my purse pretending to search for car keys while waiting for him to leave.

As I exited the examining room, I seemed to enter a vacuum. I couldn't breathe and was floating forward through the empty corridor. When I crossed in front of Dr. Kaye's office—where I knew he sat—I turned my head away, attempting to deny his existence. This denial was challenged before I could escape into the reception area.

As I neared the door, Dr. Kaye's voice resonated behind me. I glanced over my shoulder and saw that he had stepped into the hallway and was grinning. I felt a connection at the sight of him. An unstoppable warmth arose from my core and climbed into my head and across my face in the form of a blushing smile.

He'd said something about a safe trip back to Austin.

Gushing, I responded, "Thanks, I will see you."

At the check-out desk, I pushed the warmth away, gave the receptionist my name and went about with the business of being a patient. By the time I arrived at Love Field and boarded the Southwest 727, I could no longer ignore the warmth and feelings churning up with ever growing intensity. I selected a window seat so I could turn my body and appear to be focused on the world outside.

At the first opportunity, I ordered a Chardonnay. By the second sip, tears were rolling, and by the second Chardonnay, I bawled in silence as I realized what I felt.

I'm in love with Dr. Kaye.

I was 30,000 feet in the air and on my way to meet Trey in Colorado to celebrate our 29th wedding anniversary. Alone within myself, a plastic cup of Chardonnay, the infinite sky, and the earth below, I acknowledged the sorrow in my situation. I did not judge myself. Nor did I think about what I should do, or how I would be affected. I just kept moving. *Forward Progress Always!*

Before landing in Denver, I pulled myself together and proceeded as planned. First to baggage claim and then to catch a shuttle to the offsite rental car building. I had just enough time to stop by an adjacent gas station before heading back to the airport to pick up Trey.

I was famished and, due to tear-induced sodium depletion, craving salt. With no healthy options, I grabbed an oversized individual bag of Lays potato chips, which I emptied while watching Trey's plane land via a flight-tracking app on my phone. I had no thoughts of Dr. Kaye and my earlier realization as I sat in the dark rental car eating potato chips for the first time in years.

Deny, numb, and carry on.

The closest I came to saying anything that weekend occurred during dinner the evening of our anniversary. The bottle of Riesling we shared had unburied my truth by the end of the meal. As Trey made one last toast, I was hit by a wave of guilt and started crying. The only words I managed were, "I don't deserve you."

The truth was sitting ready in my throat, but all I would let out was, "I don't deserve you," which I repeated through the tears. Trey attempted to console me by affirming his love and assuring me that I did, indeed, deserve him.

I wonder what chaos would have ensued had I the personal strength to speak my truth that evening of our 29th wedding anniversary?

Regardless, chaos was inevitable.

Chapter 12
FROZEN

Well before moving Mom and receiving my diagnoses, Trey and I purchased one of those resort promotions that offer rooms at super cheap prices if you agree to sit through a sales pitch. We would have normally tossed those types of promotions, but this offer was from a resort in Maui – five nights for just over five hundred dollars, and we could schedule the trip anytime over an eighteen-month period from the time of purchase.

We had never traveled to Hawaii, nor had we vacationed anywhere without our daughters since they started school; meaning kindergarten. The decision to purchase the deal was easy and we'd amassed more than enough airline miles to get us both to Hawaii; we just hadn't known what all we would be facing over the course of that year-and-a-half.

The five-night stay had to be booked and completed before January 2012. That didn't happen. After a sympathetic booking agent and her manager allowed us to extend our booking window, I mustered up the courage to ask for more time off work, and we departed on Leap Day 2012, for what felt like an actual restful vacation.

Our first morning in Maui, Trey woke up with a renewed energy and spirit that I hadn't seen for some time. Some of whatever weighed him down had dissipated in his sleep. He was lighter, as if the Hawaiian air had swept his soul of obstacles, and the island's beauty had opened his mind to seeing possibilities.

I was happy to experience this more positive and open Trey. He was much more fun and we loved hiking, snorkeling, and even swimming in the ocean. Never had I been comfortable swimming where I could not see what dangers lurk nearby; yet, in Maui, I let Trey coax me into deep water. I loved the feel of the salt water against my skin, but remained apprehensive. Several times I told Trey to stay in front of me, but I never defined where "in front of" was and he assumed I wanted him to face me. I kept circling to take in the varying scenes, and Trey followed to assure he always faced me. Feeling exposed when he was not in between me and the vast unknowingness of the open ocean, I became frustrated and bellowed, "Stay in front of me!"

"I am in front of you!"

I confessed, "No! Shark-side!"

He laughed with me and at me as he repositioned himself.

This trip offered an opportunity to begin those hard conversations and settle old betrayals. Instead, we chose to keep those doors shut and focus on fun.

Maui was a turning point for Trey and his health, however. His new zest for life was naturally accompanied by a desire to preserve that life, to finally start taking care of himself. Being immersed in Maui's beauty and it's fresh-from-nature food sources helped him to accept the direct relationship between his health and the food he put into his body.

I was happy to support Trey and his new eating habits. But, his first step toward change and the encouragement it brought were not effective in eradicating what had already firmly taken root and lived within me. What had sprung forth from the seed of gratitude remained— perhaps to sustain me—a substitute for the pain and a filler for the holes I failed to recognize. I don't know. The feelings persisted, anchored securely under my skin, both feeding and consuming my soul. They surfaced from my subconscious at various times – on hikes in Maui and on the Austin greenbelt while trying to keep pace with the heels of Trey's Keens as they took on a life of their own. Trey was there – present only with the beauty of the nature surrounding him and unaware that, in my mind, I was hiking with someone else.

On movie dates, the person I imagined sitting next to me would have never subjected me to darkness and violence. No, he would have taken me by the hand and led me out of the theater as soon as he noticed I did not like the movie. And to escape the chaos of my house, I'd wonder why Dr. Kaye mentioned the possibility of a "home visit" and envisioned what that might entail.

Looking back, I see that I checked out during situations in which I failed to use my voice; situations where I failed to practice self-care; and situations where I found it easier to escape in my mind rather than speak up or take action to make the actual escape my inner self desperately desired – a practice honed in childhood as one of those self-preservation skills.

These skills had served me well to stay attuned to my dad's shifts, my mother's distractions, my siblings' taunts, and the overall temperature of my house. Like a marvelous internal machine, it was a contraption mix of thermostat, radar, and compass all synced and forever recalibrating— showing me the best words, the best routes. During significant time swaths in that bio-dome of Wichita Falls the perceived best route was often inside my own head creating worlds where my true self and rampant imagination could be released without repercussions. They were worlds where I'd gain senses of wonder, security and significance.

• • •

Rejuvenated physically, I returned from Hawaii optimistic about what my life and relationship with Trey could look like in the future. Although our messy, hidden spaces remained unexplored, we did acknowledge our mistakes of not making time for fun and not embracing and immersing ourselves in nature's beauty. Not that we could have afforded such a trip previously, but there certainly was no shortage of unexplored hiking trails, swimming holes, and wonders of nature in the central Texas area.

My return to work coincided with a need for increased focus on the research study. Earlier in the year, I had stepped into an unexpected role when the contract writer refused to conduct a series of presentations outlining the study's structure and progress. The writer ended up leaving the project altogether sometime during my week in Hawaii, so I assumed the role that should have been given to me in the first place, had I not faced an unknown fate, multiple surgeries, and Mom's decline.

Sweeping aside the lessons learned and best intentions we had set in Maui, Trey and I threw ourselves back into work and settled down into our comfortable ruts. Although an April post-operative appointment loomed—the fourth, and a six-month milestone—work demanded my attention, accommodating my denial of feelings for Dr. Kaye. At least outwardly.

When I was engaged with work, people, and reality, I had no problem staying present. But when alone, my mind floated away with the feelings: alone during nightly soaks in the bathtub that Trey encouraged and enabled, perhaps because he needed the time alone in order to go down his own rabbit hole; alone during dreadful morning and evening commutes; and alone as I lay down each evening, turned off the light, and closed my eyes.

My thoughts and feelings for Dr. Kaye came to be like medicine—a secret drug I relied on—that made me feel euphoric the same way morphine had warmed my soul and protected me from feeling the deeper truth of pain. *Who best to administer good medicine than a doctor?*

My perceptions of how Dr. Kaye had behaved—his smiles, his stepping out of his office and watching me leave, his nervousness while leaning in close to remove stitches and wires, his strange reference to April being "hh-oo-T!," the long awkward stare—fed my thoughts and feelings. Perhaps all these instances were misperceptions – perhaps I had made them into what I wanted them to be; into what I needed.

• • •

My jaw seemed to be healing at a slow rate while numbness lingered around and below the right side of my mouth. Yet, I resigned to treat the April post-operative appointment as more of a nuisance. An attitude that negated the natural fears I would have, had I been willing to acknowledge and discuss my circumstances with Dr. Kaye. I was not that person.

Instead, I was the person who felt completely torn as I sat in front of my work computer contemplating the impending appointment. A part of me desired the freedom and the opportunity, should it arise, to explore the feelings and get answers. Another part of me questioned the questions, rationalized the feelings, and accused my other self of complete absurdity.

As I pulled up Southwest Airlines' website to check flight options, the internal struggle ensued. My deep feelings and my rational, yet guilty, brain found a compromise they could agree upon… using the excuse of needing to attend an afternoon meeting in Austin, I would catch an early morning flight to Love Field and take a taxi to the 8:30 a.m. appointment. The compromise was booking an immediate return flight, allowing no time whatsoever to explore or discuss, much less acknowledge, my secret truth. A truth that had grown despite—or perhaps because of—my refusal to accept and verbalize it.

In passing, I told Trey of my plan for the appointment, and he instantly accepted it as the most logical and efficient option – I had made great healing progress, and our lives, routines, and work priorities had taken back over – why would he object? I didn't question my plan, and my external façade helped to convince my internal self that, *Yes, I'm just making a quick trip alone, up and back, for a routine check. It's a bother really, and I'll return immediately following to make the 'important' afternoon meeting.*

• • •

The sun rose as the Southwest jet's wheels lifted off the ground, leaving behind the world I knew well and in which I felt perfectly comfortable and safe. It was a crisp, clear morning in the high 40's. I was very aware of the weather, since I had been hoping for such a morning – beautiful and cool, as it should be. It was mid-April and it was not "hh-oo-T!"

I folded up my olive green trench-style jacket, and tucked it between my right leg and the armrest. The jacket's belt was too long to buckle and was meant to be tied, which I considered a weird fashion trend, but I was glad to have the jacket with me – a non-verbal defiant statement, and some self-assurance, that it was definitely not "hh-oo-T!" No, it was a cool and gorgeous April morning, and all was as it should be.

The spring had brought some much needed rain to Texas, and the patchwork of greens below reflected its positive effects. They were colors not seen on the Texas landscape for some time, and I escaped into them as they sparkled and changed with the rising sun, and with each new series of fields that approached and then slowly passed from sight. The greens provided beautiful focal points, and while disappearing into them, I released ownership of my feelings along with the real reason I was alone in that plane.

I retained the state of detachment as I entered Office Building One and ascended the great staircase. There he was again, right on cue, the "man at the top of the stairs" with cell phone in hand.

After checking in, I sat down in the waiting room for only a few moments before my name was called. At the door stood the same nurse who had flashed me a concerned look after measuring my blood pressure during the previous appointment. Unlike my adeptly trained and forced persona, my vital signs were not capable of masking nervousness, fear, and truth.

Breathe.

I entered the examining room, placed my purse in the empty corner chair, and laid my olive jacket over the chair back as statement to both myself and Dr. Kaye, *See, it's not hot in April.*

While the nurse finished up with her checks and questions, Dr. Kaye entered the examining room. We exchanged smiles and handshakes as he acknowledged the necessary travel from Austin. "You did get up early this morning!"

"Actually, I flew."

My intonation contradicted the point of his statement but my words hadn't. Realizing this, I reached within for my safety net—my beautiful green fields—and rambled about how lovely Texas appeared from 20,000 feet. The awkward chatting fizzled out soon, and the routine exam commenced.

While Dr. Kaye completed the exam and proceeded to go over his canned statements on timelines and expectations, I stopped listening. I gazed at him as words I did not hear came from his mouth, and for a sliver of a second, his eyes met mine. In that fraction of openness, my eyes revealed that I was beaming on the inside.

As he headed into the hallway, he turned and paused, holding the handle of the half-opened door. Smiling, he looked at me and said "What time is your return flight?"

A warm grin swelled across my face, and my damn right index finger, over which I had no control, rose and pointed at him. "Eleven."

He exhaled, turned toward the door and lowered his forehead onto it in what I perceived to be frustration or disappointment. With a hesitant chuckle, he said, "Okay, we'll let you out of here on time."

The nurse then accompanied me into the x-ray room for another round of panoramic shots. With all guards and pretenses battened in place, I returned to the examining room alone to wait for the results.

Dr. Kaye opened the door only enough to enter. He held my x-ray printouts in one hand while his other hand attempted to close the door behind him, but the nurse was trying to squeeze her way inside. He revolved and moved his empty hand onto her shoulder. "It's okay."

She pressed forward. "You sure? Are you going to be okay?"

Laughing, he guided her out of the doorway and assured she was not needed. My astonishment at witnessing this exchange was outweighed by the searing question as to what had precipitated it. *How could he not be okay? What does she think I'm going to do?*

The matter at the door got settled, and I was alone with Dr. Kaye – a prospect that suddenly mortified me. He turned from the door, still smiling, with his eyes lowered. His gaze followed the length of my frozen legs and moved up my torso before settling horizontally. Our eyes met again and he gushed with a grin encompassing the entire lower half of his face.

I took that as the opportune time to ask about the numbness around my lip and chin. As I spoke, my hand rose to my mouth to point to the area, but before finishing my question, Dr. Kaye swept the x-rays down and across his chest. "Stop that!"

His command seized both my breath and words. *Stop what? What do you think I'm talking about?*

Taking a step back he said, "Now, is there something you want to discuss?"

Some part of my subconscious knew he was referring to the tension between us. But I was in a deep state of denial, so my brain reacted by disassociating, protecting me from what I perceived to be threatening... my truth. A vacuum surrounded me impeding my ability to breath. He was waiting for my answer – *please stop smiling like that* – so I grasped onto the dental chair's arms to keep my hands in place. The room blurred as I clung to consciousness and focused on the illuminated end of the black tunnel where Dr. Kaye stood waiting for my reply. "Will... my cheek... eventually heal?"

Still gushing, "Yes."

"And... the area around my lip and chin?"

Laughing and nodding, "Yes."

"Thank you. That's it."

With the x-ray images still in hand, Dr. Kaye moved behind me to a workstation and the examining room's white walls reappeared. I exhaled as he seemed to give up on discussing our situation. "Well your x-rays look good. All the screws are in place and there's no new bone growth… your body likes it."

I stiffened further at this remark. His unusual selection of words provoked thoughts unrelated to the medical device implanted in my face. I remained petrified until my brain forced reason. *He's referring to the implant; it's not being rejected.*

"Great!"

Dr. Kaye said something while moving between the workstation and my left side. He was tapping a pen on one of the x-rays, so I shifted and turned toward the image as if I was following what he was saying. My gaze focused on two staple-looking marks glowing from within my right cheek. Since the first set of post-operative x-rays, I had been curious about how two staples came to live inside my head but I never asked about them. I didn't inquire this time either. I was completely frozen.

Dr. Kaye stepped back around in front of my chair and leaned onto a wall for support as he wrote on a clipboard and once again informed me of the timeline for future follow-ups. The appointment was over. With relief I lifted my legs from the dental chair and onto the floor. Dr. Kaye approached me with an extended hand and I noted his grip as we said goodbye. He released my hand as I rose to standing. Before I had a chance to retreat to the corner where my purse and coat awaited, he drifted even closer, our faces drew near, our eyes locked, and he stated, "You can return to normal activity."

My heart kicked into overdrive while my stomach tightened and jumped into my chest. I had no idea what he was referring to, but the spectrum of possibilities terrified me. As they had sounded in January, his words were not odd within themselves, nor out of context. But their timing had again placed them on the extreme outer edge of contextual.

On its own, my right hand flew up between our faces and I whirled my body around and away from his. "Oh, I have."

With one leap I was at the chair retrieving my jacket and purse. When I turned around to leave the examining room, Dr. Kaye was gone.

Once again, I turned my face away from his opened office door as I passed. Approaching the lobby door, I heard someone step into the hallway behind me. I couldn't bring myself to turn around. I was too afraid to face the eyes I felt watching me walk away. Tinges of disappointment and sadness washed over me as I entered the lobby – disappointment in myself and sadness in the situation.

Those feelings were quickly quashed and numbness once again ascended upon me as I checked out at the reception desk and headed outside to call a taxi. While I dialed, the sun's rays heated my shoulders. It was much too hot for a jacket.

With the senses of disappointment and sadness still in check, I arrived in Austin, phoned Trey, and asked him to meet me for lunch. To admit to myself that guilt had me calling Trey would have required acknowledgment of its cause. Those buried emotions were too much, too hard, and too unknown.

Perfectly comfortable and safe, I was back in the world I knew well – the world where I knew what to do, what to say, and how to act.

PART FOUR

NOT PROCESSING EMOTIONS

Our emotions merit the upmost
respect; embrace and dance with
them, but only after carefully
determining their origins
spring from truths, and
not from perceptions
or assumptions

Chapter 13
THE BUILDING STORM

Six months passed before I had to face Dr. Kaye again. I carried on with life as usual, keeping up with work and home, while maintaining a cordial relationship with Trey. Inside me, however, a storm was building, just as hot air rises and meets cold air in a turbulent swirling dance. When alone, I engaged the warmth when it rose up, then cooled it with reasoning, maintaining a calm demeanor while in my known comfortable world.

This calm, rational side questioned the warmth. *How could I love him when I don't even know him?*

One day I looked up the subject of love on the *TED Talks* website and found Helen Fisher's video, "The Brain in Love." I had not known there were neurological categories for love. I knew I loved Trey, so why were my feelings for Dr. Kaye so different? Dr. Fisher's explanations on the differences between deep attachments and romantic love described exactly what I had been experiencing – my hyperventilating episode in January, my out-of-control blood pressure in his presence, sexual thoughts and the euphoria they stirred inside.

Further research brought balance to this new knowledge. I learned there is a psychological basis for falling in love with one's physician. Transference.

It's the same psychological basis for falling in love with anyone. The subconscious brain identifies someone as fulfilling what it has been programmed to search for at its most rudimentary level, where the survival instinct exists and directs the newborn to nurse. These fundamental feelings of the need to survive, of love and attachment, are first projected onto parents or parental substitutes. Whether you want them to or not, they then can be projected onto other people your subconscious brain identifies. And whether we want to or not, we humans fall in love with our rescuers.

Almost all of what I found on transference was relevant to psychiatric-based, physician-client relationships; however, two references of occurrences between medical-based physicians and patients were enough to console myself that transference was what I was experiencing.

It also made perfect sense. I lost my mother during the time that Dr. Kaye came to my medical rescue. I had convinced myself that Dr. Kaye experienced similar feelings. He had told me that "our youngest son" left home for college. He, too, had a void in his life. But since I was unwilling to have that conversation, I really didn't know Dr. Kaye's thoughts and feelings.

I found solace in my newly acquired Google knowledge, as I was glad to put the "transference" label on my feelings and discount them based on a psychological phenomenon. It enhanced my arsenal of cool logic used to build resistance to and rationalize away the deep warmth, at first anyway.

By May, the warmth mounted a full-frontal counterattack to logic, and I needed to release some of the escalating pressure generated by my internal storm – to share my experience with someone, like a long delayed exhale.

A problem with people who have highly developed self-preservation skills is that they do not ask for help. They refuse to, because at some point in their life, they learned people cannot be trusted. Not even those the rudimentary part of their brain first identified as being fundamental to their survival.

• • •

Susan is four years older than I am and was somewhat of a surrogate mother. Before her teen years, she looked out for me and allowed me to be a part of her world; and I welcomed her into mine. On one fall morning cool enough for coats, we walked up the alley behind our house on Westward and shared a package of graham crackers. I told her of the alley's magic as we walked.

The first section, the one directly behind our house, was "Grassyland." The knee-high grass turned golden in the summer and its ends looked like caterpillars. I placed the ends between my forearms and rubbed them together to get the "caterpillar" to crawl up my arm.

The next section was "Rosyland." The redwood fences that bordered it were covered with climbing rose bushes that became so weighted down with red blooms that their branches draped over and onto the ground. I tried sitting under them once, but the thorns were not friendly.

The third section was my favorite, "Honeysuckleland." It smelled the best and made me feel the happiest. The bees seemed to prefer it, too, but I did not mind them.

Last came "Jungleland," which began where the navigable part of the alley ended. Its bordering fences allowed only enough room for weeds to grow. I was never brave enough to squeeze into "Jungleland."

After Mom's death, Susan and her husband resumed their navigational loop around the earth, which limited our communications to a few emails necessary to settle Mom's estate. Her son's May wedding presented the first real opportunity to talk. They docked their boat in St. Maarten and flew into Baltimore a few days before Trey and I arrived.

We met her daughter at the airport and she rode with us to a beach house on the Delaware shore. Catching up with my niece and hearing of the wedding plans was a nice distraction. Times like those, in which I was fully present, provided relief from the turmoil that crept closer to the surface. Helping Susan with flower arrangements and setting up reception tables were also fun, welcomed distractions.

During a break, I asked Susan if we could talk. She was glad to and also needed to visit. We retreated to a quiet living area in the beach house and settled on a loveseat facing each other. I had not rehearsed or even contemplated how I would approach the subject, I just felt like I was going to burst. To have the turmoil not live solely within me, I needed to tell somebody. I didn't want to gain a different perspective or seek advice. I just wanted and needed to say, *Hey, this is happening to me.*

As we sat down, the words that came out of my mouth were, "It hasn't been helpful to me that we haven't had Mom's funeral yet." I then sobbed as the next words—what I had actually intended to say—swelled upwards into my throat.

Before I could release them, Susan was crying, too. "Me, either."

Since her return to the boat following Mom's death, she and her husband had had issues. Susan had decided to take a break from their marriage once their trip concluded the coming July. She was very upset; understandably so. I listened, consoled, and offered support.

I don't recall whether I decided not to add to her burdens by not sharing mine, or if we just ran out of time. It doesn't really matter. Our conversation ended with an agreement to begin planning Mom's burial and funeral services, and with my building storm still swirling inside me.

My rationale on moving ahead with Mom's funeral service was that I had fallen in love with my doctor because my mother had died, and that the delay of her burial had caused those feelings to remain and grow. I thought burying her ashes, along with funeral and memorial services, would fix me.

From the point of my failed confession to Susan, I hung onto that hope. Hope strong enough to keep the swirling dance contained, but not powerful enough to keep it from building.

The pressure at work was mounting as well because the timeframe to finish the research study had narrowed to less than four months. I had become a human pressure cooker. In a frenzied attempt for relief, I contacted my siblings and the National Cemetery to arrange Mom's burial plans for as soon as possible.

Susan, her husband, and their boat were scheduled to arrive in the Chesapeake on July 4th. Peter wanted Mom's side of the shared headstone to be engraved with her information prior to the funeral service, but the National Cemetery would not order the engraving until the burial had taken place. Ed had no requirements, and I was simply trying not to explode.

Six weeks prior to the funeral date, I again boarded an early morning Southwest flight heading to Love Field. This time carrying my mom's ashes in the urn Susan and I had selected eleven months earlier. Although not an official service, I was required to schedule a specific time with the National Cemetery for the burial.

After landing, I had just enough time to pick up a rental car and drive to the cemetery for the 10 a.m. burial. The friendly retired veteran who had helped me schedule the burial was waiting. The plan was for me to drop off the urn for the cemetery staff to bury on top of Dad's coffin.

He sensed my reluctance to hand Mom over and invited me to walk with him to the gravesite. A gorgeous morning with a few clouds scattered about the blue backdrop of a sky, the sun was slow at warming the day. The veteran boasted about the cemetery's beauty on the walk as I wondered about my brother, Ed. I had emailed him to let him know the time of Mom's burial and invited him to join me, but had no idea if he would be at the cemetery. He was not.

Two groundskeepers with shovels stood waiting at Dad's gravesite. They had done a nice job. The hole was perfectly round and centered in front of Dad's headstone, just wide and deep enough for an urn. A round tuft of grass and the pile of dirt waited to return to the earth.

I kneeled down and placed Mom in the hole, then picked up a double handful of the loose dirt and let it fall over her urn. The groundskeepers took over with their shovels and I stayed until they filled the hole and returned the tuft of grass to its original spot. Through a few tears, I said goodbye to Mom and apologized to her and Dad for her burial, such as it was.

After thanking the veteran and the groundskeepers, I returned to the rental car, and headed to a shopping mall. The next day was Trey's birthday. Since I was already to be in the area, we made last minute plans to celebrate his birthday with dinner that evening and spend the following day in Arlington at Six Flags Over Texas.

Finding the perfect gift for Trey took no time, and I left the mall to check into the hotel Lindsey had recommended for its historical charm and location in the quaint Elmhurst area, just west of the DFW Metro Medical Center. After dropping off luggage, I set out on foot in search of food. Strolling along the sidewalks aligning the busy streets of Elmhurst, the buried warmth in me became hyper-aware of the proximity to its source

Both a desire and fear of seeing Dr. Kaye plagued me. Elmhurst had no shortage of luxury vehicles, and each one caught my attention. I stood on the threshold of an all-out panic attack.

Is that him? Will he see me?

Shit, that's him! No, it's not!

That's him, that's got to be him!

Deep within my brain, a desperate searching mode had been triggered.

Will he stop and say hello? What will I say?

Fuck, that's him!

No, that couldn't be him!

My heart raced. The air thickened, and I couldn't breathe. Dark cars seemed to be surrounding me when I felt a gentle tug on my purse. The strap was slung over my right shoulder, and I jerked my head around to the right. No one. I whirled around to the left. Again no one.

Clarity came along with a voice of reason… *Go back to the hotel and eat.*

Once at the hotel, I calmed myself while eating and waiting for my family to arrive for what ended up being a fun-filled weekend.

• • •

Back in Austin, I returned to what had become my routine. During the long commutes to work, I allowed fantasies of life with my rescuer to take over my brain, but transitioned back into reality after parking my car and walking into my office building.

The lingering effects of the feelings of love, hope, and yearning had awakened a new energy in me. I exuded authentic confidence at work. I stepped outside the bounds of my perception of how I was expected to conduct myself, and instead began shooting from the heart. I spoke with authority and without apology. I stated my opinions, and people heard and heeded them. I researched and wrote an entire section of the study in two days.

I'm a machine. This is the real me.

Through twelve-hour workdays this energy sustained me. The fantasies resumed on the commute home, and the lingering chemicals they created carried me through the remaining evening until I went to bed, where the fantasies took over again.

This was my new life. The unexpressed and embattled warmth and cool within me had created two separate selves. It was not a healthy routine, but I had no power to stop it. It felt good. I needed it, and I thought, *It will all be over once we have Mom's funeral.*

Closure requires funerals. That is what I had always heard anyway. I just had to make it six more weeks until August 10th – a full year and three days after she died.

Chapter 14
THE BATTLE AGAINST THE STORM

Nothing changed following Mom's services. Trey and I resumed our comfortable rut of a routine, our garage and spare bedrooms remained impassable, and all overstuffed closets and cabinets remained unopened.

At work, the research study's report took shape and was completed by its September due date. The focus moved onto communications and legislative strategies, and I was more than up to the tasks as my thoughts and fantasies of love generated an excess of feel-good chemicals to keep me fully charged. I had become a full-blown addict by this point, and my rational self was weakening.

The date for the one-year post-operative appointment loomed next, but logic told me I should not see Dr. Kaye again. Changing doctors would require an explanation. I would have to voice what I was pretty sure Dr. Kaye already knew – my feelings. Or was it *our* feelings? In my fantasies, the feelings were mutual. In reality, maybe he believed I was special. *Someone had to think I was special.*

For the past 12 months, reflections of Dr. Kaye's past behaviors—his nervousness, incessant smiles and glances, the tension and awkwardness— had fertilized the seed of gratitude I planted. As the date of my next appointment neared, my mind turned from the fantasies to the questions, seeking a solution to the impending appointment.

My two internal selves negotiated. Both had good points...

You're not really in love with him, it's only transference.

No, I love him! I think he tried to kiss me.

No, he wouldn't have! He's married! You're married!

He knows! He knows I'm in love with him and he's in love with me!

Ridiculous! But what does "You can return to normal activity mean?"

Yes, that was so strange! Was he trying to take advantage of me?

How could he know how you feel? There's no way he could know!

He does! And I need to talk to him about it. I just don't know how.

He'll think you're crazy. You're acting like a silly schoolgirl!

As the arguments lasted through the early morning hours, a clear winner never emerged. I operated on two to four hours of sleep, yet felt completely energized, more than energized. It felt as if I had entered a sphere of energy, like the air I breathed and the space I walked and drove through had a palpable mass. I noticed and felt everything and everyone.

Billboards and bumper stickers breathed new meanings, every song on the radio was an affirmation of *our* love – the *signs* were everywhere and could not be disregarded[1].

The sight of luxury cars, particularly dark-colored BMW's, disrupted the fantasies during my morning and evening commutes. Certain cars stood out, same as they had the day I buried my mother. As they approached, my heart raced because it seemed not only feasible, but also probable, that Dr. Kaye sat in the driver's seat.

Under the thinning shell of my skin, I searched for him. Both of my selves sought him – one with yearning and the other with fear. The quest only stopped once I arrived at work or home. Clarity came with the work I loved. In the evenings, I escaped the reality of my home by retreating to my study to spend hours scouring the internet for answers. *Why had my right condyle grown at random, and now, why does my left one feel like it's growing?*

---

[1] Finding meaning and connections in random things or events is known as Apophenia

• • •

The Texas Longhorns played their second 2012 home football game in early September and Trey wanted to go, so I went along as usual. As we walked with the crowd toward the stadium's entrance, I kept an eye out for Dr. Kaye. *He's probably driven down for the weekend to watch the game or for some parents' meeting or something.*

As the throng of burnt orange fans compressed to enter the stadium, I scanned over the top of the crowd checking for salt-and-pepper hair. Within the mass of air and space, I could feel him and knew I'd run into him somewhere, sooner or later.

Two older gentlemen sat across the aisle to our left about twenty feet away from our seats. They appeared to be brothers – round friendly faces, neatly dressed in white business shirts tucked into belted khakis. The man seated nearest us wore a fedora-style hat. Our eyes met as I sat down and he lifted his hand to his hat and nodded with a smile.

They seemed out of place. They were calm, content, and quiet while surrounded by an orange sea of excitement and madness. As the game commenced and as I pretended to be engaged by it, I felt their presence— like they were watching me.

The Texas side scored on their first, second, and fourth possessions, prompting regular cannon blasts that shook my soul and lifted me out of my seat, despite the fact I knew to expect them. By the third score, the gentlemen were on their feet. Instead of exiting on the stairs that separated our sections, they crossed into our section and were squeezing their way down our row. Trey and I stood to make room as they approached. The man who had smiled was the last to pass. As he did, he paused in front of me, looked into my eyes and grinned with an understanding nod. His reassuring eyes sparkled as I returned the smile – I sensed he knew what was going on inside of me.

I later pointed out to Trey how odd it was that they never returned to their seats. He only vaguely recalled the two men and was puzzled as to why I thought the occurrence was significant enough to mention. I let it go, but the smiling man's face had been imprinted in my brain.

And I would see him again.

• • •

The evening following the Longhorn game, Dr. Google revealed symptoms of a condition that aligned with what I had been experiencing. Acromegaly in adults causes facial bones to grow, along with several other more common symptoms, including many I experienced such as fatigue, sleep apnea, and ocular migraines. The bone growth and other symptoms occur as a result of a tumor on the pituitary gland, which causes excessive amounts of growth hormone to be released into the body.

Over the course of the next several days, another self emerged to intervene in my internal battle. At last my brain had something else to focus on and obsess about. There was not enough bandwidth to worry about the impending appointment with Dr. Kaye. The likelihood of another tumor offered a more palatable prospect than my truth, and this new self embraced that prospect wholeheartedly.

For three days, I mulled over the new explanation to my left jaw pain without considering how the symptoms were a convenient distraction and possibly the result of my internal battle. To acknowledge either would have given credence to the truth.

Sitting in front of my work computer following a meeting in which I was both present and not, my rational self expressed the last thoughts it would have for some time. *Is this pain real? Could I be sick again?*

I closed my eyes and ventured inside to what I felt physically. My left jaw joint throbbed. *Yes, it hurts; something is going on with the left side of my face.*

A surge of panic rippled through my body and something clicked in the center of my brain. *I'm sick! I need a doctor! You can't be anything to me but my doctor!*

I tore up all the notes and poems I had written, erasing all physical evidence of anything otherwise, and logged into my DFW Metro account to send Dr. Kaye a message. I had to tell him my left jaw was growing and warn him that my upcoming appointment was not going to be routine. I typed a convincing note about Acromegaly and my related symptoms and hit send. My message was rejected for containing too many characters.

I tried decreasing the words without reducing "credibility" and hit send a second time. Rejected again. After the third attempt failed, I decided perhaps technology was acting in my best interest, and maybe I shouldn't send such a message. I picked up the phone and dialed Dr. Kaye's office and left a message for him to call. I then contacted my local primary care physician, explained to her nurse that I had Acromegaly, and requested a referral to a neurosurgeon, which she oddly did not question.

Next I called DFW Metro's neurology department for an appointment, but was told the referral would have to come from another DFW Metro physician. I contemplated my options. The thought of Dr. Abbey's nurse came to mind. She had been nice and helpful during my parotidectomy.

I need to call her! She will help me.

My call to Dr. Abbey's office was patched into her current nurse. She was also friendly and receptive to my concerns. Calm as I relayed what I was experiencing on the left side of my face, I made no mention of Acromegaly. Perhaps enough time had passed to allow my initial panic to subside, or maybe it was because I was communicating with the DFW Metro Medical Center and their computer had already rejected the notion three times. The new nurse set an appointment for me to see Dr. Abbey the next day.

After hanging up, I contacted Trey to let him know and ask if he would accompany me. Of course he would.

That evening, I compiled a history of my various Acromegaly symptoms, a sort of side-by-side comparison that pointed to only one logical conclusion: the one supporting my self-diagnosis and justifying the level of my concern. After Trey convinced me to come to bed, my ruminations continued. Instead of sleep, I drifted into a type of resting state where all conscious brain functions shut off, except for the one trying to sort out my dilemmas.

Before the sun rose, I headed into my study to work on the symptom list again. By the time it was perfected, it was three single-spaced pages. *Dr. Abbey is never going to read this. She's going to think I'm crazy.*

So I worked up a one-page "Symptom Summary." Still convincing, but readable, plus I would have the detailed history as a back-up. I finished up the summary just as Trey stirred. A few minutes later his feet brushed across the dining room carpet behind me.

I refocused my gaze from the words to the computer screen's reflection. The light was such that it mirrored my study's French door entrance, the dining table beyond the doors, and the floor-to-ceiling windows through which the morning light shone. Between the study doors and dining room table, stood a clothed male figure with his back to me, looking out the window.

I smiled. "Good morning, I'm almost done here." No response.

"Trey?"

Again I focused on my monitor's reflection and did not see him, nor had I heard more footsteps. I called out his name once more as I swiveled my chair around, stood up, and walked into the dining room. He was not there. "Trey?"

I headed into our bedroom and found Trey sound asleep in our bed. Only seconds had passed since observing the figure's reflection, but it wasn't Trey's.

The incident sparked my curiosity – *we are going to help you* – and provided me enough of a break from the obsessing to realize I needed to stop. I walked back into the study, printed out the summary, folded it in half three times, slid it into my purse just in case I needed to share it with Dr. Abbey, and stepped into the shower.

• • •

I didn't need the list. I had only explained a few of my symptoms to Dr. Abbey before I realized I was rambling and probably loosing creditability. I cut straight to the chase. "I think I may have a tumor on my pituitary gland." Seeing the look on her face, I spouted more symptoms to justify this belief.

Dr. Abbey calmly placed her hand on my arm. "Stop."

She then told me I needed to stop consulting the internet for medical advice, even though I never mentioned that I had been.

Images of my brain and head from a previous CT scan were already pulled up on a monitor, and Dr. Abbey flipped through them at a fast pace. I had a disk at home with the same images that I had perused for the last several evenings. Radiologists make mistakes. They don't see what they're not looking for, even condyles that resemble bent pinky fingers.

The examination began and ended with a nasal endoscopy. First, Dr. Abbey sprayed a numbing solution into each nostril and then slid a long lighted scope up my nose that flexed down into my nasopharynx, the area behind my nose and above my pallet.

The popping noises started up straightaway. "Popping in Sinus Cavities" was a symptom on my list, but not one I was particularly concerned about.

"Your pallet is spasming."

That noise is my pallet?

The popping noises had been occurring for years and at times were loud enough for Trey to hear. Following the removal of my right condyle, they had temporarily disappeared along with my frozen shoulder and other bothersome maladies.

The spasms warranted closer review. "My nurse will give you a call to schedule an MRI and follow-up appointment."

"Okay, thank you."

She then reminded me to stay off the internet. "If anything is going on, we'll address it."

• • •

A day and half passed since I had left word for Dr. Kaye. I started Friday morning with an assumption that if he were to return my call, it would be that day. I kept my cell phone next to my computer keyboard and carried it with me on trips to the printer and bathroom. All through the night I had rehearsed what I was going to say and carried on the conversation in my head while working.

I started experiencing symptoms in June… I've seen a physical therapist and neck specialist… I just thought you should know that something is going on with my left TMJ…"

All morning I was ready for his call, but it did not come. Just before the lunch hour, I carried my cell phone into the executive conference room. Our Executive Director had scheduled a last-minute meeting with the research study team and would be attending via conference phone. An actuarial method cited in our study report had been questioned, and we gathered to assure consistent understanding and responses across the team.

Leading the explanation required complete focus. I was ready – along with my cell phone, I had a clear understanding of what I would be defending. The conference call had been underway about five minutes when it was my turn to speak. Everyone understood my explanation, and a general level of acceptance had been achieved that no mistakes were made.

I was in the process of answering a question from the Executive Director when my phone vibrated. A quick glance showed it was Dr. Kaye. I froze mid-sentence... then, "I'm sorry, I have to take this call."

That behavior was not the usual me. I would have never taken a call during a meeting or even carried my phone into a meeting. The Universe was trying to act in my best interest, like when it saved me from sending Dr. Kaye a panic-induced tome about Acromegaly.

The unexpected conference call, along with the timing of Dr. Kaye's call, should have kept me from forcing the conversation I was compelled to have with him – a conversation that allowed me to avoid the one that should have taken place instead. With my phone in hand, I walked out of the meeting through a side door into a small, secluded hallway. No longer ready for his call, I hit the green answer icon and lifted the phone to my left ear. I hadn't talked on my right side since the parotidectomy. "Hello, this is Martha."

"Hello, this is—" and then a click. My left cheek had hung up on him! This had happened more than once–*another symptom!*

"Shit!" I was horror-struck and moved from the hallway into an empty breakroom. While I dialed his office, my phone vibrated again. "Hello, I'm so sorry!"

I told him what happened and then segued into the reason for my call. As I blathered on, my pounding heart crept into my throat causing my voice to crack. Still, I refused to give up control of the conversation. He spoke through my rambling, but I ignored his words. They were not on the same level as my forced conversation. His words were on the level of truth that I refused to recognize. With a tone of compassion, he'd whispered, "It's okay."

But to me, it was not okay – it was not even close to okay.

Chapter 15
EMBRACING DARKNESS

My focus had changed, leaving me no space to be in love with Dr. Kaye. I had a tumor, I could feel it. During our phone conversation, Dr. Kaye mentioned I could move up my one-year post-operative if I felt a need.

Of course there's a need!

A tightness stretched from the left base of my skull, up through my head, behind my left eye, and out my forehead. With pressure and throbbing in my left ear, jaw, and glands, I thought, *it's happening again.*

An MRI and follow-up appointment with Dr. Abbey were scheduled for late September. I called Dr. Kaye's office to reschedule my post-operative appointment for the same day, narrowing the timespan in which I would have to face him.

Work flowed in slow motion. I kept calm and focused, and spoke only when necessary. Primarily, I observed. It is amazing how much more one can see while existing within an energy sphere where the mass of air and space can be felt. I had long known the personalities and tendencies of my co-workers, but for the first time, I saw what was driving them – their insecurities, perceptions, and desires. I was merely filling a role in an elaborate play, and had just awakened to the fact that that is where I had been all along – acting with everyone else, letting insecurities, perceptions and desires direct me.

That awareness did not matter at the time, however… *I am dying.* And I slept as the prospect of dying had resolved the need for my other selves to engage in battle.

• • •

Rounding a corner on the way to the examining room we encountered Dr. Kaye. At the sight of him, cool logic lashed out, *Yes, Trey's with me — you have to be my doctor!* Once settled into the dental chair, my warmth stirred and threatened to expose me. In a weird effort to suppress it, I bundled up my sweater and placed it over my lap like a shield.

Dr. Kaye entered soon after and took a seat on his stool at my feet, his face void of color.

Trey broke the silence. "How's your son?"

A wave of relief washed over Dr. Kaye's body and deposited a smile across his face. A genuine one, like those I had witnessed during previous inquiries about his son. He was glad to connect to the love and fulfillment that glowed at his son's mention.

No, Trey does not know.

I participated in the banter. Play acting, except I was the lead actor and all my selves were aware I was acting. My third self was still in control though. It had to be. I had a legitimate concern for my health which required maintaining the act while explaining my recent symptoms. Aware that my situation was cause enough to question the symptoms, I prefaced my description with, "I know this sounds crazy, but…"

I hate that phrase. I hate that any person would ever feel the need to discount their thoughts and feelings, and essentially, their self. I hate that I did. But my third self insisted as it balanced the acts of denying truth, maintaining decorum, and seeking medical assistance all at the same time.

Dr. Kaye delivered his quick response with a tone of compassionate disagreement. "No."

I didn't look at him, nor did I stop talking. It was not in my script to acknowledge anything else I perceived as crazy. He was aware that an MRI was performed that morning, declaring, "Along with the MRI our regular examine will reveal any changes so there's no need to stray from the usual routine. Let's start with the x-ray."

I stood and began unscrewing the diamond stud earrings that Trey had given me the Christmas before and that I had worn for his benefit. Dr. Kaye studied my hands as I placed each earring into Trey's open palm. He then lifted his gaze to look at me but I refused eye contact.

The panoramic images were consistent with the previous x-ray. Dr. Kaye flipped them around to show me and pointed with a pen. "See, your condyle's not growing." Slight annoyance had replaced the compassionate tone.

Dr. Kaye moved the rolling stool into position and took a seat. Looking up, he transfixed on my outstretched legs so I adjusted my sweater which seemed to revive him. He forced his eyes shut and pressed his left fist into his forehead as if trying to push a thought back into his brain. "Uh… I believe the sources of your pain are the muscles around your left jaw… a common occurrence in single jaw joint replacements."

Empathy returned to his voice. "The inflammation and pain are exacerbated by a vicious cycle that began with clinching. Clinching causes swelling and pain, which triggers stress, which provokes more clinching… greater pain… and more stress, and so on."

Although I knew I wasn't clinching, I went along with his theory because I had no argument for the "vicious cycle" component. In fact, those words described exactly what I was experiencing in my mind.

"A custom-fit mouth guard will assist you with abating the clinching. It's inserted between the teeth at night and supports the muscles while you sleep. Your Austin dentist can fit you for one. I don't have to do it."

• • •

The appointment ended without my selves having to align and

acknowledge all their truths – a successful denial of the state of my being in its entirety. Successful enough anyway – Trey had no clue. As for Dr. Kaye, I had a potential medical solution, but I had failed in my attempt to hide both my warmth and fear.

Dr. Abbey's report further relieved my medical worries. The MRI was clear; I was not dying. I was glad to let go of the worry and the mental mountain, that third-self my brain constructed. Fear had taken control, and I let it reign over me.

Death was doable; verbalizing my feelings was not.

I had a clean bill of health and a cushion of twelve months before I had to face Dr. Kaye again. Trey and I left for Austin without returning to the BMW dealership we had visited to kill time between appointments. Trey had insisted we stop and test-drive a small sedan. I assumed he noticed my fascination in the vehicles and was trying to please.

I didn't want a BMW. That event, and the entire day, had served as a wake-up call. I needed to get help and resolve my feelings. I didn't trust them, and I didn't want them.

A few days after the appointments, I contacted Grace, a therapist who specializes in grief and life changes. I had long known I needed to share what was going on inside of me. It had become more than I could handle alone. It was my full intent to reveal my truth and seek guidance when I filled out the paperwork, submitted it, and confirmed the date and time of what would be my first-ever therapy session.

As the number of days before the session shrank, that rationale eroded. The notion of exposing my truth stirred up the internal storm. Again, cool logic was determined to win. But that level of denial required re-engaging fear, so I stopped sleeping as my mind ruminated on questions and searched for answers...

Do I really love him? Does he love me?

What the fuck does "you can return to normal activity" mean?

Why did he look at me like that before my surgery?

What was he doing while my back was to him?

I replayed every encounter in my head over and over, dissecting and analyzing every statement, gesture, and eye contact, then obsessing over those that could not be clearly categorized.

What was that? That made me feel uncomfortable… that look made me feel uncomfortable. No, it scared me. He scares me.

Within the week, fear gained control again. The mental mountain was back and had convinced cool logic that my troubles were solely the result of Dr. Kaye's behaviors.

Perspective shifted. The nuances of our interactions that had supplied me with copious amounts of adrenaline, dopamine, and serotonin took on different meanings. The man my mind had become addicted to was now a threat.

• • •

I sat down on the loveseat in Grace's office, a small converted space adjoining her garage. A large window with sheer curtains provided a generous source of natural light. Filled bookshelves lined one wall, her desk and chair the other, and matching loveseats in floral upholstery occupied the remaining two, leaving just enough space for a tasteful Persian rug.

I thought of my mother.

Right away Grace acknowledged that I had been through a lot in a short period of time, so I knew she had read the form I had filled out seven days prior. I'd listed "transference issues" on it, but that fact had since been evicted from my memory and Grace didn't mention it.

My first appointment consisted of reviewing the history and dynamics of my family, the one I was born into. I had always had a clear perspective of what my family was and was not. I was the youngest of four children, an unfortunate birth order in a Marine household where vulnerability was an open invitation for ridicule. Like all humans, I carried the residue of childhood traumas into every interaction, but those traumas were not the prevailing issue. They were, however, driving my fears.

Grace did not mention "transference" in my second appointment either, scheduled three days after my first. Instead, she listened as I recited the encounters with Dr. Kaye that I was obsessing over – the ones I had not been able to assign clear meanings to as well as the ones that had previously brought me warmth, but had since turned scary. Scary, like dying, was easier than my truth.

Grace sympathized and questioned me on what motives I believed guided Dr. Kaye's "behaviors." I couldn't answer. Those were my big questions, what I had obsessed over.

That he had scared me was obvious to her. We scheduled another session for early the following week, and she walked me the three steps to the door and held it open as I left. I thanked her, and she assured me we would figure out what had me so frightened. She then mentioned she specialized in hypnosis techniques which could be useful in helping me sort things out.

My fear moved into DEFCON 4 at the mention of the word "hypnosis." *What does she think happened to me?*

By the time I sat down in my car to drive home, my fear had concluded that she thought I might have been hypnotized. *She must want to hypnotize me to find out.*

It had already been a full day. That morning I left work after Lindsey called me in hysterics. She had just learned that a car had struck a close friend, killing him. My daughter needed her mother. On the drive home from Grace's, one of my brothers called. I didn't know exactly what he was angry about, something built on perception. Perception has too much power, and the power he gave to someone else's Facebook post blindsided me. I had no idea what he was talking about, and he had no clue of what I was going through.

My bedtime rumination routine went into overdrive that evening, creeping further into an irrational, paranoid realm. All the questionable interactions that were rewinding in my brain connected, making more sense. Interactions I had not previously questioned came into play and helped with constructing a bigger, darker picture.

Dr. Kaye had told me, "We are going to assault you." He woke me up during the surgery; he said he would test my facial nerves. With his face directly in front of mine, he'd called out, "Martha, Martha."

Did he?

Yes, he said "Martha, Martha" right in front of my face... inches from my face. The angle... he could have only been on top of me. *He was on top of me when he said that... there was no one else around...* I only saw him.

He had checked the healing of my scar in January, the first appointment I attended without Trey.

Why did I want to go alone? Why did I feel so drawn to him? I had to have been hypnotized... *he must have laid out the entire plan when I was under anesthesia...* there was no one else around when I saw his face hovering over mine.

He could have easily drugged me in January. Did he have gloves on when he rubbed my scar? He was behind me. I couldn't see what he was doing. He rubbed his finger along my scar. He could have been applying a sedative to my skin, like the ointment I had for Dad when he fell into hallucinogenic rages. *Dr. Kaye's must have been stronger... he knows how to sedate people... he has drugs for it.*

Why did I feel like I was supposed to go alone? He must have told me to… it was part of the plan, his plan. 'You can return to normal activity.' *That must have been the trigger phrase to wake me up.* 'He means sex!' I instantly thought of sex because that must have been what just happened. *My brain was trying to tell me!*

He said that April would be hh-oo-T! *Why did he think April would be hot?* It's never hot in April. *He had to have known what would happen at the April appointment… what happened in April?* He pushed the nurse out the door. He waved his hand… he told me to 'Stop that.'

He said, 'We'll let you out of here on time.' *Who was 'we'?*

He told me, 'Your body likes it.' *Likes what! Why did he say that?*

'You can return to normal activity.' He said it again at the end of the appointment.

It was out of context. It wasn't necessary. 'You can return to normal activity,' while invading my personal space. I didn't know what he was talking about! *Sex acts?* I threw my hand up between our faces. The thoughts that thudded into my brain scared me. *Why? What happened in April?*

The man at the top of the stairs! *Was he a lookout? Had he been on the phone with Dr. Kaye letting him know I had arrived alone?* He was always at the top of the stairs! *Was he part of this? He must have been watching for me to show up without Trey.* It was just a matter of time… *it was part of the plan!* That's why I felt I needed to go alone. That is why he had entered the procedure room in November – he had looked around to assess the situation. *The man at the top of the stairs is in on it! Did he rape me, too?*

Why did Dr. Kaye try to refer me to a plastic surgeon? Was that his friend? Was he trying to pass me around? Who was 'we'?

Dr. Kennedy! She hated me. *Why did she hate me?* Why do women treat other women like that? *She must have witnessed Dr. Kaye's attention.* It aggravated her and she took it out on me. *She wanted to show me I was not special…* she told me I wasn't special!

Dr. Christopher! He scanned my body. He told me Dr. Kaye was the only person who could help me. *Why did he say that? Why did he want me to go to Dr. Kaye? Was he in on it?* 'He has to accept you.' *Accept me for what?*

Was the plan more than just Dr. Kaye's? Did it all start with Dr. Christopher?

Dr. Augustine! He was aggravated with Dr. Kaye. He didn't like what was going on. He came into my room in the dark with a flashlight… he just checked my wires. Meredith was there. He asked if Dr. Kaye had been by yet… *was he checking on me? Dr. Augustine must have known what was going on… he didn't know what to do.* He was okay… Dr. Augustine was just checking on me.

My lip had been cut!… there was a stitch in it… no one told me about it. *Why had the corner of my lip been cut? Did Dr. Kaye implant something in it?*

Why are staples inside my face? Am I being tracked? Is this how he's controlling me… controlling my thoughts?

My body lay still throughout the night, relaxed in a sleeping state while part of my brain separated and seemed to operate in another dimension where it could search non-stop for pieces of the puzzle.

Chapter 16
LOST IN DARKNESS

The mass of space and air grew even thicker making it difficult to move through as I walked, yet it seemed to support me at the same time, keeping me upright. I hadn't slept in days but it seemed as if I were the only one awake, the only one aware. Trey sensed I needed to get out of the house the weekend following Grace's "revelation" that I had been hypnotized.

We'd restarted the renovation projects, and I wanted to complete the finishing touches on our bedroom. I was on a mission to find the perfect bedskirt, even if I had to sew it myself. Trey didn't really care about bedskirts, but he knew I did.

Warm for early October, it was a beautiful, sunny weekend for shopping. The man was extraordinarily tall, the kind that towers over others and that everyone notices, except no one seemed to be. His fit upper torso, neat black hair, and ivory face hovered above fabric bolts three or four aisles away.

He was at the last store.

As we left, I asked Trey, "Did you see that tall guy? He was at the last store we were at."

"What tall guy?"

We set out for a nearby shopping mall and Macy's household department. The lights were almost too bright, and colors abounded – rich, deep, vibrant colors.

A group of three women huddled at an intersection of four aisles. We had to step around one of them. Well before we approached the group, I had noticed her. She stood out in her old-school athletic shorts, yellow with white trim, and the classic runners completed her 1976 look. I followed Trey around her and onward through the mass, and we departed Macy's empty-handed. I had found the perfect color bedskirt, but it was not the right size.

As we left, a pair of neon turquoise sweatpants caught my attention as a young, slim black man arrived at Macy's exit with us. When he passed by, I turned and examined him. His gaze focused straight ahead as he pushed through the doors to the outside. The day was too warm for sweatpants, and it was not the right decade for neon turquoise ones.

Trey was hungry. I no longer needed food. The same energy that allowed me to function without sleep fueled my body. Despite considering it a nuisance, I agreed to stop at his favorite Mexican food restaurant before heading into central Austin. Well before Trey, I finished my meal and excused myself to go to the ladies' room. We were seated in the bar area, and I wound my way around a dividing wall toward the bathroom. There she was, sitting in a booth with the other two women, still talking. She and her old-school shorts and tennis shoes stood out again. I stared as I approached the booth and walked past. She never looked up nor stopped talking to her friends; she carried on as if she did not notice me.

But I knew she had... *she's here because I'm here. She's watching over me.*

The second Macy's did not have the bedskirt. Nor did the third, and as we exited through two sets of glass doors, the same young man with neon turquoise sweatpants entered. His gazed remained locked ahead, even as I studied him as he brushed by.

The unsuccessful mission had taken most of the day. Within one afternoon, in a metropolis of a million-plus people, three individuals had appeared in two separate locations each. None noticed that I had crossed their paths twice, and each had seemed out of place.

Although entwined in my dance with fear, these individuals didn't frighten me. No, at a time when the mass of air and space seemed to be the only thing keeping my legs from collapsing, the odd individuals who appeared throughout my day had comforted me. Logic and hindsight suggest such occurrences are not so uncommon, and I was only aware of them due to my hyper-vigilant state. However, the encounters had consoled me – *we are going to help you.*

I am not alone... *were they angels?*

Those beliefs brought me no relief from the ruminations that had taken over my nights. Just as during the last ten months, when my head hit the pillow, my brain left it – going to a happy, sexy place that fueled my days. That place had since become dark, where conspiracies and evil conjoined. Each time, my brain had gone just where I wanted it to go. Like when I disassociated in Dr. Kaye's office, my brain was abiding – trying to protect me from my deeper truths by drifting into another dimension.

> Dr. Kaye... stands to the left of the dental chair with his back to the wall and next to the closed door of the examining room. His right leg is bent and his foot is propped on the wall – like he is waiting.
>
> *My eyes flutter open.* He gazes at me with a smile, nodding, and takes a step toward me to shake my hand. The appointment is over... I get up to leave.
>
> *No. He was on my right when I got up to leave.* I tried to ask about the nerve damage to my lip and chin... he said, "Stop that!"
>
> He stood looking, smiling, and nodding at me. *I got up to leave. Dr. Kaye came toward me – he grabbed me by both shoulders to support me... I was dizzy, confused. He helped me back into the dental chair.*
>
> *I had gotten up to leave* – he had been to my right – but no, I remember getting up and he was on my left, leaning against the wall... he had smiled and nodded.
>
> *My eyes fluttered open as if I had just awakened.* He came toward me to shake my hand... "You can return to normal activity."

But he had been on my right. *He helped me back into the chair… someone burst through the office door! The man at the top of the stairs!*

My body lay still while my mind trolled the depths of my subconscious. The images it conjured scared me. My left frontal lobe ached and an energy charged through my nervous system and settled into the left side of my body. The energy roused me. Conceding, I rose at 5 a.m. and headed into the bathroom to shower. My breath grew heavier with each step and my entire body trembled. Without switching on the light, I leaned back and my hips found support on the counter.

What's happening? I was frightened and tried to rein in my breathing. *Who's there?* A presence stood nearby… in front of me… inside me. *What's happening?* The walls were spinning around me. I was descending. Some force pulled me deeper into darkness, a vortex. I strained to maintain a connection to sanity. *Help!*

I rolled around to the sink, lifted my hand to the wall and found the light switch. *No one's here. What just happened?* I was scared and shaking. Through muffled sobs I leaned over the sink until my forehead touched the mirror. Peering deep into my eyes, I prayed aloud to what I sensed lay beyond their depths. "Please… help me!"

Somehow I drove to work while the night's images cycled and recycled through my mind. Pulling into the parking garage, I spotted our Human Resources Director's car. *What's he doing here so early?*

On the walk to my office building, more ruminations connected and led me to conclude that Dr. Kaye must be under investigation by the FBI.

They've discovered he's conducting mind control experiments on his patients. The FBI asked the HR Director to come in early to inform him that I'm a victim. They're going to confront me and tell me what happened.

The creepy new auditor and I reached our building's secured entry at the same time. He was an ogler and had recently moved to the office across from mine. *Is he part of this? He's always watching me.*

Sitting at my desk, I tried to focus on work, but *the FBI is coming downstairs soon. They'll want to know what I remember.*

As my new memories rewound, I tried to make sense of them:

Dr. Kaye was on my right when I got up to leave. Then he was on my left and I exited the room again. I left twice. *How does that happen?*

The FBI and HR Director are upstairs preparing – they'll be down any minute. They're going to help me. *I was part of a mind control experiment, but they suspected Dr. Kaye took it too far. He had raped me in January, and forced me to perform set acts on him and the man at the top of the stairs in April.*

This is what happened! This is why I have two memories of getting up to leave in April. *I was drugged before the first attempt.* I remember – I could see Dr. Kaye to my right as I stood up, *and he took me by the shoulders and sat me back down.* Next, I saw him leaning against the wall waiting for me to wake. He shook my hand and said, "You can return to normal activity!"

This is what happened and everyone knows it. The HR Director, the creepy auditor, and the government officials upstairs. *This is what they're getting ready to tell me.*

My heart raced. I couldn't see. I was slipping again, farther into the dark vortex. Fighting for air, I wondered if Joanne, my co-worker and office neighbor, could hear me. *Joanne! She's my friend. She'll help me!*

Between gasps I whispered, "Joanne…"

Then louder, "Joanne… Joanne… help me!"

My chair was pushed out from my desk and I was hunched over my knees, quivering. Joanne appeared at my office door as my torso started rocking back and forth. Between huffs I exhaled the words... "He raped me... I was drugged... and he raped me. I left twice... I got up to leave twice! I remember getting up to leave twice."

"What? It's okay. I'm here."

"Help me."

"Is there someone I can call? Who's your therapist again?"

I pulled Grace's card from my purse and handed it to Joanne. She closed my office door, called Grace and left a message. Joanne was a calming presence, and my body downshifted from rocking to trembling. She stayed with me while I phoned Trey. "I'm okay... I just need you to pick me up now."

I don't know what Joanne and I discussed through the duration of the wait—small talk, I suppose, to distract my brain until my phone rumbled with Trey's text, "Here." She walked me downstairs and out the door where I collapsed into Trey's arms. I clung to him hoping to disappear into his chest. I wanted to be tucked away inside him and not have to wake up from my self-induced nightmare.

• • •

Because I was "in crisis," Grace worked me in that afternoon. I relayed my fears to her, fears related to doctors anyway, nothing about mind control experiments or the FBI. Logic had returned somewhat. I did tell her about Dr. Christopher informing me that Dr. Kaye had to "accept me," so she may have sensed my suspicion of a bigger conspiracy. Again, she listened and discussed maintaining a yoga practice and grounding exercises.

I left her office with an index card of phrases such as:

"I am safe."

"I am grounded."

"I wrap myself in a protective bubble."

"If there is something more to remember, my subconscious will let me know."

I was to refer to the phrases and concentrate on them instead of allowing ruminations to take over my brain.

My inability to accept and speak my truth—what was going on inside of me—had led me into the darkness. It's heavy in the dark. You can't breathe. The darkness had accommodated both my denial and my fear. Darkness was what I wanted it to be – a place where my feelings made sense and my questions were answered. I had searched for the darkness and entered it willingly. But it wasn't until the power of its vortex drew me farther into its depths that I tasted true fear. I lost myself to the dark, and it was up to me to find my way out.

I held no concept of light at the time, but I had a strong will, yoga, and an index card with four handwritten truths.

PART FIVE

NOT ACTING UPON YOUR TRUTH

Truths have their own energy and leave
indelible marks on the Universe and
our Souls—regardless of how hard
we try, or how far we run,
we cannot escape their
all-knowing energy

Chapter 17
SEEKING LIGHT

The greatest challenge following the breakdown was battling my brain's default mode to ruminate. *I am safe. I am grounded.* In the evenings, I couldn't turn off the part of my brain that had engaged fear. The battles ensued into the morning hours. Exhausted, I was not winning.

During a half-sleeping state, I had a dream-like experience, more of a flash dream, a vision that lasted only a second. A hand clasping a cloth and surrounded by light appeared in front of my face from the right. Its strange appearance came so suddenly and clearly that my entire body shuddered. The shock was quickly subdued by a deep peaceful state that fell over my body like a mystical healing blanket, and I slept for several hours.

The next morning I arose and stepped into the shower only a semblance of the person I had once been. My body felt like it had been plowed over by a steamroller with thick aerator prongs that left gaping holes over its entire length. I could feel all my holes. I had nothing left to fill them.

I am safe. I am grounded... what does that even mean?

With no success, I looked at my feet and tried to sense their contact to the shower floor. I turned toward the water that fell in front of my face, hitting the center of my chest. I lifted my hands together at my heart in prayer position, except inverse, with the length of the back of my hands touching, leaving my palms open. That is what felt right.

The streams of water shimmered with reflections of the bathroom lights. I focused on the dancing rays of silver and gold until I could see nothing else. An overpowering light swelled up from within me and conveyed new mantras that I recited through tears… "I am love, I am light, I am hope, I am joy. With God's love and light, I am love and light."

Over and over I repeated this until I gained the strength to carry on with washing my hair and soaping off.

Later I stopped in at work to make an appearance and assure everyone I was okay. I requested and was granted use of personal time for the remaining week. My mind was in recovery, enough anyway, and it needed to rest. With a one-week pass to take care of nothing and no one but myself, I booked a mid-week spa day.

Trey returned to work. He was concerned, but we did not talk about why or what had happened.

• • •

Upon arriving at the lakeside resort, a sense of relief washed over me as the driveway gate closed. I had entered a safe zone void of anyone from whom I had to hide my true thoughts and feelings. I changed into the robe and slippers provided and headed outside and downhill toward the water.

A stone wall with square openings, like large windows, lined a portion of the path halfway down the hill. The openings provided a view of the sloping lawn and flowing river below. I stepped over the shrubbery dividing the path and wall, sat down crossed-legged on the ledge of the middle window, closed my eyes, and breathed.

For the first time since my mother died, I lifted my face to the sun and absorbed its energy to the accompaniment of birdsongs. The pain in my left frontal lobe released, the mass of the air thinned, and I was conscious of my own presence.

My brain was fully with me for the twenty or so minutes that I sat. When I opened my eyes, the grass, trees, water, and sky were as they had been before, just cleaner and crisper, like my vision had been out of focus and then recalibrated with my breath and presence.

My eyes followed my feet to the ground as I stood. Next to my left foot lay a smooth black rock discarded among the blades of grass. It resembled the river rocks used in massages. I picked it up and rolled it around in my palm, noting its weight and density, then lifted my fingers open. Shaped in the form of a human heart, this was a strong heart, and mine was not. So I slipped the rock into my robe pocket to remind me of where I needed to get.

The massage therapist detected my holes, grief, and exhaustion. She warned me I might experience emotional releases during the massage.

"What do you mean?"

"Our bodies hold onto unprocessed emotions. Sometimes massage can trigger their release."

I had two such releases. The first came in the area of the surgical scar on my neck, and the other was in the area of my clavicle of the same side. In both instances, a swelling of great sadness lifted from within me, but with no specific events or thoughts attached. The pain surfaced and burst out of my body in a series of heaving sobs. Maybe it had just been waiting for permission.

The therapist also sensed the sources of my exhaustion. "You have two energy vampires. Those are people that feed off your energy, it can be all consuming."

She left me with advice similar to Grace's, only instead of visualizing a protective bubble, she said I needed armor. "Joan of Arc armor."

Even though I was not physically endangered, the state of my being was. I was a walking open wound, and needed armor, like adhesive bandages, to keep foreign particles from entering and causing further harm while I healed from the inside out.

Following the massage, I sat alone in a tile-lined cell surrounded by a fog of eucalyptus-infused steam. Sweat and tears poured from me as I spoke to the connections I felt. I succumbed to my truth and a sense of overwhelming love. I spoke aloud to Dr. Kaye and I spoke aloud to God.

"This is more than I can handle. I don't know what to do. I'm not ready. I need to figure this out. Please, help me."

• • •

My sister and her husband arrived in Austin the following day, a Thursday. They had purchased tickets to ACL a couple of months prior and we made plans to attend with them.

I had since slept three nights in a row and my brain and body reaped the benefits. I had contemplated the vision of the hand and cloth and determined that the cloth was for me. In the evenings when the frightening thoughts replayed in my head, I visualized the cloth wiping them away... *I am love, I am light, I am hope, I am joy. With God's love and light, I am love and light.*

Soon after she landed, I met Susan at a café in East Austin. I felt good and was happy to see her. It was easy to talk to her and relate what I had attempted to tell her five months earlier... I had fallen in love with my doctor and had not told Trey. I acknowledged my transference research, assuring her I knew how and why it had happened.

She appreciated and supported my points on the psychology of my situation, as did I – they explained and provided an acceptable label for my feelings. I was still wide open, but no longer in a dark way.

The light was working, and the music and crowds of ACL were nothing short of magical for this hyper-vigilant music lover. I roamed through gauntlets of people across a mystical playground collecting Universal secrets while set lists, lyrics, and a rotund tie-dyed belly with the words "It's Not Time" fed my apophenia.

EXORCISM BY FLORENCE + MACHINE

Anamorphic colors sweep over crowds
Surrounding me
Encapsulating me with protective light
Words, carried on waves
Piercing my body
Reverberating in a purifying baptism
Romance, regrets, and devils
Extracting my soul
Swaying and swirling I dance
Barefoot over beaten grass blades
Syncing hips to tambourines
Stomping feet with drumbeats
Into a powerful crescendo
Jumping with 50,000 strangers
Twirling in spontaneous tribal revelry
I feel my devils
Surging through my body
Levitating higher
With each liberating leap
Bursting out of my raised palms
Sweeping away
Into the ether

Trey's enjoyment was not near the same level as mine. Around my sister, he didn't act like himself and he never gracefully accepted not being the center of my attention. Already anxious, his sense of solitude within the comfortable rut heightened his insecurities. I had been thrown from the rut and was not capable of going back – the rut was synonymous with death.

In the days following ACL, I had trouble verbalizing this to Trey as I continued to heal. Somehow I would have to share my truths with him in order to find a way forward. I thought about all I had experienced – the scary, the strange, and the beautiful. Truth—what was inside of me, but what I had been conditioned to think of as expendable—forced me forward. I thought about Jesus, or at least what little I knew about him. He was a man with a truth though, a truth from which he did not waiver in the face of death.

I've never been able to fully embrace the concept of deities, but the association of Jesus with Truth was profound, a truth in itself sprung from an inherent knowing... *I'm supposed to follow my truth.*

Many others in human history had followed the examples of Jesus, or those of their own personal prophets of truth. Gandhi, Mandela, King, Parks – all had held steadfast to a personal truth. *The deepest level of who I am, the level beyond fear and all that is derived from fear, is sacred.*

Truth is sacred.

• • •

The weekend following ACL, Trey and I sat together undressed in bed. I had waited for him to awaken while rehearsing various scripts, all with the same bombshell ending. All I initially managed to say though was, "I need to tell you something."

When it came to actually telling Trey what was going on inside me, all my words disappeared. Openly discussing an ugly truth, displeasing the ones I love, and exhibiting honest fragility all in one conversation, went against every instinct imbedded into every molecule in my body. I couldn't do it, I couldn't say the words. So Trey began to ask questions, "Have you fallen in love with someone else?" was his second, after "Are you leaving me?"

The "with who?" part of the Q&A was not as successful. After grossing me out by naming a couple of our neighbors, he pressed on. When his head, shoulders, and chest slumped inwards toward his heart, it seemed he'd figured it out. He spoke slowly in a defeated tone, "It's a woman, isn't it?"

I was stunned and responded with irrepressible laughter. That was a terrible thing to do, but it was just so funny! Here I was tortured by my truth and in turn was torturing Trey through a silly game of 20-questions. Although he was serious, his concern—which I guess from a guy's perspective is one of the worst things that can break up a marriage—added a bizarre levity to the scenario and forced me to finally speak up.

"No, no," I assured him. "It's just Dr. Kaye, my surgeon. It's called transference... it happens between patients and their doctors."

He was understandably hurt, but he wasn't angry. And because of my tendency to paint the rosiest of pictures possible, the way the admission unfolded helped me to downplay the true depth of my feelings, and avoid the subject of my state of being. My mental health wasn't even on the radar as we moved straight to the "how did this happen?" part of the conversation.

I told him I had been unhappy for a long time and I told him why. Trey was familiar with all the whys—all the matters we had left unresolved over the decades. He admitted that he knew I had been unhappy. He was hoping it would pass, which is what one does in preference for the comfort of ruts over the discomfort of truth and the unknowns associated with that truth.

• • •

The affirmations were effective during the quiet and alone times that had previously been spent ruminating. I added to them as new words entered my mind and with what was needed each day. Sometimes it was, "With God's grace, I am grace," or, "... I am patient... I am strong." Otherwise, "...I am love, I am light, I am hope, and I am joy," were the consistent mantras that allowed me to sleep.

In the shower each morning, I recited them again with the backs of my hands pressed together at my heart, absorbing the love and joy in the water's light. With time, the mass of air and space thinned, and I came to feel the shower floor supporting my feet. I had not stopped practicing yoga, which is all about connecting and grounding, but sensing my feet's connection to the shower floor was a personal benchmark because that's where I first became aware of my lack of a foundation.

Afterwards, I told Grace that I figured out what "grounded" felt like.

It was a step.

• • •

Through the remainder of the year, Trey and I spent most evenings trying to come to terms with how to move forward. It was not a productive process. Our definitions of "forward" were not aligned.

Trey carried his own childhood residues, which included abandonment at birth, an alcoholic father, and being raised at the center of a beautiful love bubble his adoptive mother constructed following the tragic deaths of her two natural-born sons. Trey had been loved unconditionally. His boyhood world revolved around him… he was never wrong, and never had to share nor compete for attention or affection. That love bubble was all he knew, so he'd constructed one around our relationship and reacted harshly toward any perceived threats to its delicate structure.

In the early years, I had been quite content within it, maybe because his bubble embodied the opposite of my childhood. Over time, however, it turned suffocating and stifled my personal growth. That is the nature of bubbles… they're limiting. Because he held no sense of it even existing, Trey could not envision a life beyond his bubble. As for me, continuing with life is it was invoked visions of my imminent death.

Although my healing progressed, the post-traumatic stress (PTS) had completely disconnected me from the woman I had been. When photos of our Hawaiian vacation scrolled as a screensaver across our television, the female in the images seemed like a stranger. I didn't know how to get back to her. At the time, I didn't know I was not supposed to.

Trey agreed to attend a few counseling sessions with Grace, "only if it would save our marriage." He had required such ultimatums before; like security blankets, they provided semblances of comfort and knowing. He needed black or white. All I had was gray, but when the cost of not attending became apparent, he acquiesced.

In the beginning, the separate sessions were helpful in opening up some dialogue between us as we hashed out with each other what we had already discussed with Grace individually. After a time, Trey came to understand that I needed "space." I knew I needed space, too, but neither of us grasped how to accomplish that effectively. Trey believed that meant simply having alone time. For me, his very existence had become enough to make me feel anxious. What he wanted and what I needed were not the same.

I was on the road to healing from my dark nights—the post-traumatic stress-related symptoms—and had gained strength in my being. Just not enough to tell Trey that I no longer wanted to be married. The incongruencies between truth and my spoken words persisted, as did my internal conflicts. While my soul screamed for change, I was laden with guilt.

After about four months of making no progress, my feelings for Dr. Kaye intensified and I was again progressing up the spectrum of PTS symptoms: intrusive thoughts, hyper-vigilance, insomnia. By Mid-March of 2013, I was on the verge of another breakdown. Something had to give, and this time I did not want it to be me.

In what can be described as both cowardly and as a desperate attempt to save myself, I took advantage of Trey's first ever "guys weekend" to escape his bubble, our house, and my home life as I knew it. Without his knowledge, I signed a year lease for a one-bedroom apartment located a few miles from my office, and on the south shore of Austin's Lady Bird Lake. After dropping Trey off at the airport, I returned home to pack. Moving through the evening, I took only what I needed and could carry. The lights from passing vehicles were almost too bright to bear, and I was again paranoid and in full-search mode. *I'm being watched – that black truck is following me. Dr. Kaye knows I'm moving; he's been waiting for me to move.*

The delusions compelled me. Within that hyper-aroused, irrational state, I found the strength to leave the inertia of my personal life and to save myself.

That inaugural morning in my new apartment, I arose for the first time in years without sensing the wrenching pull of Trey's insecurities and our messy, hidden spaces. No one I knew was privy to where I was. It was liberating to have a space in which I did not have to be anything to anybody. With enough sleep to stop the chemicals that had fueled me, my mind's state from the previous evening had healed somewhat leaving me with the weight of reality.

I was weak. I was on my own. To face that day and the unknowns of coming days, I needed strength. Real strength, not strength powered by fantasies and delusions. I picked up my yoga mat from a box and stepped into my new living room. I left the light off and rolled the mat onto the wood-patterned vinyl flooring. By pressing my feet downward I established a strong foundation and worked to balance myself in Warrior I pose. Standing with my arms, torso and heart lifted, my internal sources of strength and power ignited and burned words into my head that I spoke aloud. "I am a warrior. I am strong and powerful. God gave me strength and power to use for all things good."

For Warrior II pose, I adjusted my back foot outwards, allowed my hips to follow, and lowered my arms ninety degrees. I focused on the tips of my fingers that lay before my gaze. More words came. "God gave me vision so that I may see the path before me. I will keep my head up so I may clearly see my way."

Now I had two new mantras, mantras specific to yoga poses.

Chapter 18
ON THE WATER

I could sleep in my apartment. With no hidden chaos and no one to overwhelm me, it contained no more than what I needed. Eliminating daily commutes tempered my default modes, the incessant searching and self-soothing through fantasies. My after-work routine had been broken, and I gained control over where I steered my Tribute. During the first days after moving, I steered it to my apartment, took a seat on the rooftop deck overlooking Lady Bird Lake, and did nothing except breathe and absorb the serenity within the water.

I am hope, I am joy.

Sleep, a sense of control, and the calming water of Lady Bird Lake had the greatest effects on recalibrating the healing process.

I did not tell Trey about my move until after he returned. I picked him up from the airport and waited for an opportunity as he churned out his trip's details over the 50-minute drive. We entered the house together. I got as far as the kitchen and told him I had leased an apartment and was leaving.

The animated, happy state he had exuded while recounting his trip drained from his body. Blindsided and speechless, he stepped outside onto the patio to process. He didn't understand I was leaving that instant, but I did not follow him to explain. Instead, I turned around and walked out the front door. I could no longer be responsible for his happiness. I had to take care of myself.

Trey and I agreed to tell our daughters together. I told them I had been unhappy, and how that misery, combined with my mother's death and my medical needs, had made me susceptible to transference. I didn't mention the paranoia or other irrational thoughts because I didn't want to lose further credibility. (At the time, I didn't know my lack of sagacity was the result of post-traumatic stress.) Instead, I presented my moving as an attempt to rescue myself in order to teach my brain that I didn't need a rescuer, believing that would cease my feelings for Dr. Kaye. That was my ultimate goal, rescuing myself seemed like a logical pathway.

Meredith was supportive and seemed to relate; Lindsey was not so understanding. I wanted nothing more than to be a happy family again, but I had work to do. Trey had work to do, too, because I was not returning to what had been. That "me" no longer existed, so going back was an impossibility.

In the absence of Trey and my perceptions of his needs and desires, my own space allowed me the freedom to move forward with healing. The rooftop deck and a dock sitting over the water at the lake's edge became my healing oases. More mantras came with more yoga poses until I had an entire vinyasa series—a symphony of movements with specific dialogue—as affirming poetry.

From Warrior II, I'd lift my front arm and chest skyward for Reverse Warrior. "I happily accept these gifts from God, for which I am most grateful."

Then moving my torso forward, my front forearm to my knee, and my back arm upwards and over my head into a side angle. "I will share these gifts with all I meet so that others may know them."

Triangle pose was next, with my front arm and fingers pointing at my forward foot and my back arm lifted to the sky. "There is only one path in which I may remain a strong, powerful, visionary warrior. That path is through my truth."

Turning my torso forward and my chest downward into pyramid pose,

"I am on that path…" moving my hands to the ground to support my torso while raising my back leg behind me in a standing split, "…and I am ready to take off. I am ready to fly."

Lowering my back leg to meet my other in a forward fold, "I bow down to the will of God, the will of the Universe…" and pressing my feet into the ground to lift my torso, chest and arms skyward to standing, "…for I am of the Universe, I am of God…" then with my hands coming together at my chest in prayer position, "…and I am love, I am light, I am hope, and I am joy."

As the words came, I understood them but didn't have a full grasp on how to live by them. Regardless, the poses and accompanying mantras became part of my daily routine. While in my apartment or alone on the rooftop deck, I spoke them aloud and recited them in my head during yoga classes. Healing came. The sphere of energy—the air and space I felt—returned to beautiful, and I was a part of it. I felt connected to the Universe as the single entity it is, and relished within its joy emitted through sparkles of light that appeared against blue skies after meditating.

As I took more control over my life, the overwhelming desires and emotions for my doctor lessened. I came to view the entire situation with enough rational thought to let go of what didn't make sense… the false memories and paranoid ruminations. I sought wisdom in books, too: books that helped discern what I had experienced, on both psychological and spiritual bases; books that helped me gain a level of acceptance of it all; and books to assist with the healing process.

Through Dr. Peter Levine's *Waking the Tiger, Healing Trauma*, I identified my experiences as symptoms of post-traumatic stress. I learned of the detrimental effects of unprocessed traumas, the havoc wreaked by negative biological energies. Dr. Levine's somatic healing exercises successfully clarified long buried memories, while his expertise and insights helped me to unleash personal strengths to better guide and support my will to heal.

With Dr. Gerald May's examinations into the correlations of "darkness and spiritual growth," in *The Dark Night of the Soul*, I recognized the consistencies between post-traumatic stress growth and all the various ancient descriptions of awakening, or enlightenment, or crossing over or [insert your preferred term here]… they're all just different words used to define the same experience.

Dr. Michael Garrett's *Walking on the Wind, Cherokee Teachings for Harmony and Balance,* affirmed the connectedness of people and nature as a whole, a oneness with the Universe. The Cherokee[2] teachings shared through Dr. Garrett's stories also assisted me in letting go of the need to control, and to seek acceptance, beauty, and peace in all situations.

I was on my way, but where, I could not see.

• • •

Trey was hurting but supportive. He helped me move one of our sofas into my apartment, set up an iron rod-and-glass-top desk I bought on Craigslist, and repaired a flat tire on my bicycle. On occasion, I invited him to join me for dinner, and afterwards we sat over the water and talked. Sometimes he brought his bicycle and joined me for a ride around the lake.

The beauty and water worked its magic and his vision of what life could be broadened. After a time, I invited him to leave his bicycle at my place.

We had some hard conversations, enough anyway to move forward with the tasks of cleaning out our closets and impassible rooms, the literal ones. Trey began the work alone because I experienced panic attacks if I spent too much time at our home. At first, too much time amounted to about five minutes.

Trey also moved forward with finishing the renovations begun almost three years prior. I helped when I felt up to it. With a growing cognizance of and respect for my needs, Trey never second-guessed me nor exerted

---

[2] I am a registered tribal member of the Cherokee Nation of Oklahoma

pressure. He had gained an understanding of the space I needed.

I slept, my brain healed, and my soul grew stronger.

By July, Trey spent most nights with me, and we initiated the conversation that should have taken place before Meredith graduated from high school: What did we want our empty nest lives to look like?

The home and life that Trey had previously dug his heals into was not an option unless he wanted to be alone or with someone else. I didn't offer that as an ultimatum; it's just how it was. I couldn't breathe in our old home. It represented a life I could no longer live.

Since that was the only thing we knew for certain, we agreed to move into a larger apartment in the same complex while we figured out the rest. We, mostly Trey, worked through the summer on finishing the renovations and purging the house of our, and everyone else's, "stuff." We kept only a few sentimental items, no more than what would fit into either our new apartment or a storage unit.

During the renovating and purging, Trey came to peace with selling our house rather than leasing it out. We placed it on the market the first of September and it sold by November. We had made significant progress over the prior six months – our relationship, and most everything about our lives, had changed.

Our new ground floor apartment faced the water. The second bedroom doubled as my office and Trey used a dining room nook as his.

Life on the water was a new kind of good. We filled time previously spent in gridlock cooking up creative dishes together, and we sat and talked on the dock until the bats swooped too close for comfort. Trey biked to his softball games, and we walked to restaurants we would have never tried in our former life.

Outside his bubble, Trey exhibited a new openness and confidence. We shared in the chores, played and exercised together, and saw our daughters much more – another geography-driven benefit and the one that pleased me most.

With increasing senses of control and stability within my personal life, the PTS symptoms waned. I experienced expansion in my professional life as well. Work had been a stabilizing force, a sort of safe house, for me when the symptoms had re-engaged. Senses wide-open, I thrived in settings where my brain had to focus and my personal strength, confidence, voice, and knowledge were challenged. I am not sure I could have persevered in forging changes in my personal life without the rock of my job providing support and balance. I was my best self at work, and I loved my job.

My feelings for Dr. Kaye rose and dissipated in cycles that had no pattern, predictability, or sense. I did not beat myself up over them; I allowed myself to be sad and wrote about the pain.

I didn't tell Trey. I did not want to hurt him or jeopardize our new life. Really, I didn't have to tell him. Recognizing my melancholy, he spared both of us the distress of talking about it. Perhaps a mistake.

My feelings were not at a level that conjured internal storms. Plus my goal to overcome the transference and build a wonderful future with Trey had been established as priority, creating an environment inconducive to internal battles.

Without considering options for follow-up care, I let the October two-year anniversary date of my jaw joint replacement pass. Six weeks later, I sat in my office overlooking Lady Bird Lake on a rainy weekend and searched the internet for female surgeons specializing in jaw anomalies. I found one in Pennsylvania.

The price of avoidance was to either ignore my health needs or pay for travel and out-of-network rates. *I'm being ridiculous.*

The situation, and Dr. Kaye, wielded too much power over me because I had allowed it. *I am a strong and powerful warrior. My health is more important than my fear.*

Through the healing process, I also came to realize that my fear existed only to the extent I gave it power, and my fear had been directly correlated to the power I had granted my perceptions. My perceptions had been skewed, *perception is not truth.* Yet, when I picked up my phone to call Dr. Kaye's office and make an appointment, I couldn't make my fingers dial the number. So I emailed Grace instead. Seven months had passed since I last needed her.

• • •

Grace asked me to visualize an item that represented the entire timeframe. The first image that came to mind was Edvard Munch's painting, *The Scream.*

We went with it, and she guided me through a meditation exercise where I put the screaming image into a sack, built a fire, and then threw the sack into the flames and watched it disintegrate. A few minutes after leaving Grace, I dialed Dr. Kaye's office and set the two-year follow-up appointment. My heart raced, but I managed it.

Two days before the end of 2013, I headed to the appointment alone, even though Trey offered to come along. His insecurity and apprehensions were evident, but I did not enable them by disregarding my own needs. I did not want to add any unnecessary stress, and I needed to face the appointment by myself.

I am strong and I am powerful.

The sack I "burned" with Munch's screaming figure inside had only contained my fear. Fear was not the only aspect of the "entire timeframe," and the pieces that I hadn't burned popped up in the days leading to my appointment and during the three-hour drive.

To counter, I created my own visual exercise, changing my feelings to yellow flowers and desires to orange ones, then plucking the flowers from my brain and discarding them. The hills and berms aligning Interstate 35 were left scattered with them as I drove northward from Austin.

It was an effective exercise. I was steadfast in my being and handled the appointment like the strong warrior I was. Nothing had power over me... not fear, not perceptions, not love, not even Dr. Kaye. It was a normal, run-of-the-mill post-surgical appointment, and nothing more, just as it should have been.

I was gleeful. I had defeated my own psychology. Afterwards, I called Trey and told him how it went. Empowered, I felt no need to plant flowers along the interstate on the drive home.

Chapter 19
ON THE ROAD

Trey embraced life out of the rut. He welcomed change and wanted more. With a taste of liberation from attachments in his personal life he soon longed to rid himself of those in his professional life.

The political tentacles of Texas' state capitol affected his work and tested his moral fiber. That was nothing new; what was new was that he had options. At the start of the new year, we both met the minimum age and service required to qualify for a state pension. We could retire, and Trey was ready.

With our freedom from stuff and the weight it carried, an idea born in the previous decade—to take off a month and tour Europe—gained new breath. The idea morphed with the prospect of retiring and with Trey's enthusiasm. A month expanded into a year, then two or three or five, and Europe grew into the world. It didn't sound exhausting – it sounded wonderful. *Who doesn't want to see the world?*

"I love my job."

My reluctance had no influence over Trey's fervor. U.S. and world maps covered his office walls, and his stack of Fodor's travel books inched higher with each passing week. With animated glee—that boyish enthusiasm that I'd never learned to resist—he relayed prospective itineraries. Though I'd get swept up in his whirlwind of promising adventures, I always landed with my qualms intact. Countless conversations ran along a single line…

"Mart, we can do this! I never imagined being in a position to see the world."

"I don't know that I want to leave my job. It's not a good time… maybe after next Session."

"I can't wait that long."

"We've got another study to conduct. I've got so much on my plate that I'm already invested in, that I'm passionate about!"

"You need to do what's right for you."

…until Trey grew weary of my indecisiveness and tossed a curveball of a caveat into the conversation, "Look, I can't take my job much longer. As far as I'm concerned, I've given more than enough of my time. If you're not ready to retire that's fine, but I'm retiring in March. I'm going to travel and you can just meet up with me whenever possible."

He had given more than enough of his time; endless hours of unpaid overtime managing accounting system upgrades, fiscal year closeouts, and directing a large pool of accountants. Trey knew what he wanted, I couldn't fault him for that. But his willingness to go without me stung nonetheless. Plus, in my career, I had only recently come into my own and established a befitting professional identity and reputation, ones I had toiled decades to earn.

Conflicted, I'd look out my office window contemplating the world beyond my vision, *is something else going on out there that I can be a part of?* Each morning and evening, I observed the same buildings illuminated by car headlights trapped in rows facing east and west on Martin Luther King, Jr., Boulevard. With every day the same picture, I gained an awareness of my job's cycles – cycles within each day; cycles within the weeks, months and years. Circles, really. *Is my job another rut?*

Attachments, by their very definition, can keep one tethered to a situation, person, material object, or even a job, that may not be optimal. *How do you know until you let go?*

I remembered the promise I made to my mom when she was dying. Life had since taken over, and I hadn't thought about the promise or even what "living fully" meant. My words had not consciously driven any of the changes in my life. Yet, while I pondered my next move, I could not help but wonder if such a promise, made at such a time, had played a hand in my troubles. *Maybe I fell in love with my doctor for a reason. Maybe there's a higher purpose.*

After months of taking the conflict to bed with me, these contemplations were not the deciding factor, but they may have influenced my subconscious. Yes, I resolved to leave the job I loved based on a dream:

> It was a sunny day – fresh spring grass and emerald hills lay before us and were promising looking. Although I couldn't see him, Trey was standing with me along a dirt road that appeared golden in the sun as it cut through the distant, rolling hills. As arms reached out and handed us a large metal box, we got a glimpse of what was inside the box – a beautiful and delicious looking cake with white icing, strawberries and chocolate. We were excited and accepted the box straightaway. Our four hands struggled to open the lid, but the lock mechanism was too solid and the hinges wouldn't budge. Frustrated, we soon gave up and sat down aside the road with the box between us waiting for it to open on its own.

When I woke, my first thought was, *That's so silly – we could have just gone down that road and made our own cake!*

The decision to make our own cake together had been finalized, sending Trey's enthusiasm into hyperdrive. We planned a driving tour around the U.S.'s perimeter states, visiting sites and cities on our bucket lists, and reconnecting with friends and family along the way. We gave a month's notice, and then left employment on the last day of March 2014, precisely one year after informing Trey I had moved out.

Over the course of the next fifty-one days, we researched, bought, and tested camping gear; underwent another purging of stuff; plotted our general course around the U.S.; created an Airbnb profile; and booked spaces through the first month of planned travel – New Orleans to Acadia National Park, Maine. We learned that National Park campsites should be booked early, so the only confirmed plans after leaving Maine were camping dates. Otherwise, we drafted a wish list of cities, sites, and landmarks, along with a general timeline for returning to Austin by mid-November.

The rest, we agreed, "we will figure it out." That became our motto; the words we would live by for the coming six months and beyond.

I started a blog to provide myself with a creative outlet and to keep family and friends apprised of our adventures. We signed over the title of my Tribute to Lindsey, and traded Trey's Volvo in for a new silver Ford Escape, which I fondly dubbed the "Escape Mobile."

We also bought new fancy hybrid bicycles that could handle both streets and trails, a bike rack, helmets, and every piece of paraphernalia necessary to assure we would be prepared for all possible bicycle-related conditions and calamities. No purchases, large or small, were made without Trey's thorough researching, questioning, and trials.

Putting your life on hold is not an easy task. With the exception of a weekend test camping trip, we worked non-stop. The most challenging task was the required second property purge when our budget demanded downsizing the space of our rented storage unit.

Having recently been traumatized by an inordinate amount of other people's stuff that had consumed our home—and in effect, me—the shedding of more trinkets, trifles and trivial "necessities" was therapeutic. That was until I opened my closet. Clothes were my only possessions that emulated my true self, and I had to winnow out upwards of four-fifths of them.

A sense that I might be losing myself again lingered throughout the culling process. The closet full of designer dresses, suits, and shoes along with the hippy-chick skirts, blouses, ragged t-shirts and sandals were a form of self-expression, and I had developed a relationship with them all. The colors, textures, cuts, and necklines had reflected my style, personality, and the image I wanted to share. I'd quell the feelings of loss by assuring myself, *this is a good exercise in letting go.*

Despite our best efforts, our departure time was delayed by ten hours due to an underestimation of exactly how much stuff we had. The story of our delay was one of my first blog entries titled "Nooks & Crannies." I noted that the "big stuff" was obvious. Having sold, given away, or stored our furniture gave us a false perception of progress. I wrote,

> "It is the stuff in the nooks and crannies that you don't always fully recognize, properly deal with, or simply forget about. You know, those places where you bury things you don't know what to do with – the things you don't have a need for, but because of some attachment or another, you can't get rid of either."

These words were more than a reference to the forgotten stuff behind closet doors and in the backs of bathroom cabinets. A few nooks and crannies of my own contained things I couldn't get rid of, too. I had not defeated my own psychology; I had only again temporarily succeeded at brushing it aside. But I was going to travel the world, *we're going to be "living the dream!"*

Preparing to take off on amazing adventures, I didn't consider how nonstop travel had never been a dream of mine. My psychology, however, was somewhat acknowledged. Before departing, I unpacked the heart-shaped rock and placed it under the Escape Mobile's front passenger seat. Some part of me knew it was still needed… as my talisman, my inspiration. My own heart still ached, and I wasn't fully healed.

• • •

A family wedding in North Texas kept us from heading straight to New Orleans. We filled a ten-day gap between the end of our apartment's lease and the wedding with visits to Wichita Falls and Oklahoma, including two days camping in Oklahoma's Wichita Mountains National Wildlife Refuge, where as a child, I had first gained an appreciation for climbing rocks.

We hiked up a familiar mountain trail on our first full day and basked in the beauty at the summit. As we trekked down to plan the day's next adventure, I kept an eye on, and pace with, Trey's Keens as we navigated over rocks and conversed about something. I watched where I placed each foot with each varied step. But my left foot rolled in an unnatural direction off the apex point of a boulder, and a bone cracked. Our next adventure had been planned for us – we would spend the remaining day in a local emergency room, where an x-ray confirmed a small ankle break. Four days into our travels, we headed back to Austin and checked into a hotel.

An orthopedic surgeon confirmed that the break would heal on its own and issued me a set of crutches and a lovely black boot. The boot was to be worn for the next four weeks, until my follow-up appointment. I probably wouldn't have kept that appointment had it ended up being the only follow-up appointment I needed.

Alas, less than forty-eight hours after breaking my ankle, a damp floor caused one of my crutches to slip, and I face-planted into a wall. Another day – another ER – another broken bone. This time it was my nose.

I rebuked the thoughts tapping on my brain and whispering, *hey, do you think these breaks might be a sign?* Determination reigned, *Forward Progress Always!*

My old friend, Dr. Kelleigh, worked me in the following day, surgery was scheduled for the next day, and on the third day we headed to Fort Worth for the wedding. Neither the boot on my foot nor the splint on my nose kept me from dancing and enjoying the wedding festivities. I look both elated and outrageous in photos, carrying on as if I weren't broken even while adorned with the contradicting evidence. Only ten days had passed since leaving the foundation of our waterfront apartment, and I'd already lost solid footing. But cool logic was glad to be back on track, and we arrived in New Orleans on schedule.

I ended up ditching the boot for a brace I bought at a CVS in Montgomery, Alabama. My ankle hindered just my ability to bicycle, but only as far as Washington, D.C., where we stayed with my sister near Capitol Hill. Trey's capacity to bicycle was then hindered after his bike was stolen from outside of the National Gallery on our first day exploring.

After much frustration and research, he picked up a replacement bike in Philadelphia while I was in Austin having my nose and ankle rechecked. I flew out of Baltimore for the appointment and returned to Philadelphia the next day.

We were back on track, again.

Those mishaps were inconvenient bumps relative to the wonders, beauty, kindness, and magic we experienced during the six-month trip.

Wonders such as falling asleep with senses of warmth and contentment while camping on Maine's coastline during a tropical storm; wolves howling and barking as they ran through a ravine behind our tent in Yellowstone, and waking up to find elk calves settled around us; feeling the strength of Rainer's White River through the sounds of the boulders it tossed at will; finding beauty and life in the desolation of Death Valley; standing in awe at the bases of giant redwoods and sequoias; doing tree pose while standing inside a tree, half-moon under a half-moon, and meditating inside a cave that once served as a home to an ancient civilization.

We bicycled over the Golden Gate, around Grande Isle, along the Grand Canyon's edge, and through Zion's valley, New York's streets, Pittsburgh's hills, and the Pacific's shoreline. Our high expectations of Yosemite were shattered upon emerging from a tunnel and finding unimaginable grace spread before us. We observed the strength and mass of Alaska's glaciers, and I challenged my bravery while wilderness hiking in grizzly country, through canyon rivers, and along mountain ledges with rocky descents.

We spotted our first bald eagle in the wild, and encountered wolves, coyotes, flying squirrels, bear, elk, buffalo, moose, wild horses, spawning salmon, fowls, whales, and tiny bugs and slugs of all sorts. We live in a beautiful world, and each place we visited became a part of us. Our souls absorbed the beauty and embedded it into our memories; memories we can feel and recall at will, and memories that float into consciousness through their own volition.

Many experiences imbedded impressions too deep to simply fade away. Like when we spied a pod of gray whales from the Pacific Coast Highway, pulled over and plodded downhill between massive boulders to reach the shoreline. The spectacle of breaching whales complemented by sensations of sunbaked sand and Pacific spray was singular, momentous.

All along the roadways, we met extraordinary people: Airbnb hosts, fellow hikers and campers, park rangers, store clerks, gas station attendants, fishermen, cowboys, hippies, northern Californians, southern Californians, Native Americans, and loads of international tourists. Every engagement was positive, comprised of only kind words and generous smiles.

Through our journey while driving across the Crow, Sioux, and Navajo reservations, we also witnessed indisputable suffering – the isolation and poverty of our country's native people. Lonely shacks spread randomly along dusty forgotten backroads where neither fertile soil, hope, nor opportunity ever existed. The effects of our country's imposed injustices on its indigenous residents were evident and heartbreaking. The cyclical and residual traumas only compound those effects, keeping the cruel intentions of century-old acts very much alive and breathing today.

Although nowhere near the same level, I silently experienced my own pain… my feelings for Dr. Kaye and subsequent internal conflicts persisted. For the most part, the sites and cities we visited were beautiful distractions. Our travels were amazing and, as it turned out, necessary – memories, good and bad, are necessary determinants when plotting future courses.

So, despite the broken bones, I cannot say that embarking on an ambitious driving tour was a mistake. It was just part of a bigger odyssey, a sort of journey within a journey.

Chapter 20
IN THE COLD

Fatigue set in by Chicago, for me, anyway.

As I entered our fourth floor hotel room, a commotion at the window caught my eye. A vortex of yellow leaves danced wildly just outside and carried on until Trey arrived from parking the car. As he made his way to the window, the leaves settled. The dance was done, so I pointed out its fallen participants resting on the ground and atop the swimming pool.

I should have rested, too. Chicago is where I first sensed I was running away more than traveling. I didn't tell Trey. With our general course and timeline already set, we had stuck to our list. We'd traveled for two months, and I was tired. I wasn't practicing yoga, and I had few opportunities, and even less energy, for writing.

Once again, I couldn't talk about what I was running from. So I just kept moving. Moving while not respecting my needs; moving while losing myself; moving in spite of the subtle screams arising from the depth of my being; and moving because another beautiful distraction would always be down the road to draw my attention and provide relief from my gnawing truth.

I loved the respite times when magic and beauty abounded, and I didn't want the feelings for Dr. Kaye that arose between distractions. So, I reached an accord with my feelings. A bargain that would accept their regular appearances without too much self-deprecation because it included a plan and timeline to make them stop once and for all.

• • •

Our waning days in New Mexico coincided with an early arctic blast that kept us indoors and had me longing for Austin even more. I wanted to go home. At that time, "home" was to be a one-bedroom apartment that we had reserved through mid-December.

With only two more days of traveling and one more trail to hike, we entered Texas about a hundred miles east of El Paso near Guadalupe Mountains National Park. Guadalupe Peak's summit is Texas' highest point, and climbing to the top of Texas was a fitting way to end our travels.

The weather made the 3,000-foot ascent more challenging. The wind gusts that swept through the park's valleys and up and around its peaks seemed determined to take us out. Like most of the trails we had hiked, the final ascent was the steepest and rockiest.

As we approached the summit, a cloud settled over the peak, obscuring our view of the rest of Texas. I clung to the peak's commemorative monument while we posed for the obligatory summit photo. We signed the registry and headed straight down in the event conditions worsened – my worry, not Trey's.

The weather improved as our elevation decreased, but the pace was set. We felt upbeat with a sense of accomplishment and for me, a return of security. As we talked, I lifted my eyes from the path for only a second, but that is all it took.

My back foot caught on a rock, and the pace and gravity did not allow time for using either foot to break the fall. As I analyzed the boulder that would be the impact point for my face, I flew forward in slow motion.

Trey yelled out my name and reached me in an instant. Blood gushed from my nose and mouth, but I was conscious. Weather gear had protected my palms and knees somewhat; at least they had not bled near as much as my nose, and I was able to make it off the mountain.

Our great looping quest ended just as it had begun… with a pacing out of step with my natural flow, pitfalls, tumbles, and broken infrastructure.

Following confirmation that my second nose break did not require surgery, our return to Austin focused on catching up with family and friends, mail, and routine appointments. It was time for my last post-operative appointment with Dr. Kaye. I had scheduled the appointment from the road, after devising the plan to rid myself of the transference feelings for good.

The plan was simple and involved another mental exercise. After my appointment, I would simply take all the feelings I had for Dr. Kaye, mentally put them on a tiny boat, and set it sailing down a river to float away and be gone forever. The emotions were to flow out of me and down the river never to be felt again because I wouldn't need them anymore. With final assurances of a healed and healthy jaw, I convinced myself that I would no longer need a rescuer.

• • •

As I entered the x-ray room with the blood pressure nurse, Dr. Kaye was standing inside with another patient. I caught sight of his back as he pointed out something on an x-ray film. I studied his head, neck, and shoulders trying to convince myself, *I don't love you.*

He turned to leave with the patient but stopped as I entered. Right away, and just as any returning patient would, I said, "Hello, how are you?"

He beamed and said something to the same effect and walked past me following the patient. Just before he passed out the door and beyond my peripheral vision, he stopped and turned his gaze back to me. I wondered whether he was hoping for honest eye contact, assessing my state, or just checking out my ass.

Keeping my eyes fixed solidly forward, I stepped to the panoramic x-ray machine to be radiated once again.

The appointment was routine. As it wound down, I studied Dr. Kaye again while he sat hunched on the little stool in his white medical coat focused on writing notes. I didn't know him; not really. I observed him while playing the proper patient, and with an underlying longing to reach out. *Hello, I'm Martha. I would really like to know you better.* Yet, the three feet separating us felt like an abyss, an impossible space to breach.

The appointment ended with an affirmation that I would need no further follow-up visits, and he added, "But you know where I live in the event an issue arises." Backtracking he said, "Well, I talked to my boss, and I'll be here for at least another year."

He stated this in the awkward, shy lilt I had heard before. It was an odd statement, but I didn't ask for an explanation. He then turned to leave but paused with his hand on the door handle. He exhaled, chuckled, and with slight affirming head nods he said, "Is there anything else we need to discuss?"

The proper patient said, "No, I'm good," while my true and silent-self felt my warmth rise into a smile while thinking, *You mean the fact that I love you?*

Dr. Kaye walked out the door, and I returned to the hotel room where I found Trey still in bed. I crawled in next to him and reported that the appointment had gone well and as normal as the one prior.

I closed my eyes, placed my feelings and desires on the little boat and launched them all down my mental river—an image born through compromise with what I truly desired... to go to the water. [3]

---

[3] "Going to the water" is a spiritual, purifying, and healing Cherokee ritual involving laying naked in a river or stream.

GOING TO THE WATER

Between emerald knolls
An azure exhale grazes artic rock
Its breadth and depth in infinite release
Unfettering the unwelcome
For valiant naked souls
Discharging the distasteful
From earnest bodies
Away, Away, Away

I imagine its crystalline flow
Encompassing my nudity
Clouds forming from my mouth
Hair flowing across my breasts
I long for its icy breath to pierce my body
With sanitizing rage
Exposing my latent honesty
Adrift among its stones
Away, Away, Away

• • •

My internal reaction to Dr. Kaye's question—an acknowledgment of love that I filtered and transformed before it reached my mouth—had stirred my warmth. Cool logic intervened—*No, those feelings are sailing away... I don't need them anymore*—and helped me to stay focused on the month's cascade of errands.

A dankness covered Austin through the duration of our stay, augmenting the heaviness inside of me. By the time we packed up the Escape Mobile in Mid-December, I was relieved to be leaving Austin. Our next "home," a two-bedroom apartment in Minturn, Colorado, was to indulge us with two months of living like and among ski bums.

188 ✧ Martha J. Martin

Due to a lack of time, and desire on my part, we'd left Austin without considering travel plans beyond Colorado. The only certainty was that we were to be in Miami by mid-April to embark on a transatlantic cruise to Barcelona, but even that began feeling questionable.

Minturn is a rustic mining and railroad town located in the White River National Forest between Vail and Beaver Creek. In geography and demographics, our apartment was isolating. We were the only middle-aged residents and the only ones not working at a ski resort. We offered rides between the complex and a bus stop to kids who looked too cold for the quarter-mile walk. They must have thought we were odd, but they always appreciated the rides.

During the first five weeks, a steady stream of visitors made the isolation tolerable. Skiing, meals, and fun with family and friends were also the best distractions from the nagging memory of my last exchange with Dr. Kaye. He'd offered me one final opportunity to discuss my feelings with him, but once again my fear prevailed. So those words—my unexpressed acknowledgment of love—remained within me, pulling me back into an unwanted storm.

By week six Trey and I were alone; no more distractions, just Trey, me, and my latest internal storm. That tiny boat meant to carry away my feelings not only failed, it grew into the fucking QE2 and docked firmly upon my shoulders. I was too exhausted, both in body and mind, to endure another battle between warmth and cool logic. Nor could I brush aside the questions that seared once again. *Is this more than transference? Had I actually fallen in love with him?*

The questions amplified my brain's searching mode and apophenia, while hindering sleep and reasonable thought. The heaviness of it all possessed my body like wet concrete – I needed to escape. *I want to go home, and I want to go home alone.* Trey knew I was not myself; he knew I was unhappy. We didn't talk about it so I'm not sure if he realized why; maybe he just didn't want confirmation. As for me, the transference was again too hard of a truth to verbalize.

While napping I experienced another vision, a dirt trail leading through a thicket of fir trees. The image flashed into my head with such force it awakened me, and I knew without doubt that I would soon be leaving the trees. Some force was pushing me forward, I had no choice.

Perhaps it was easier to think that way than it was to take ownership of my true feelings. Regardless, I couldn't run from them anymore. And it wasn't just the feelings for my doctor, it was everything else I felt and was not expressing: *I'm bored out of my mind; I'm not living a life I want; I'm not using my mind; I'm not writing; there's no music in my life, no dancing, and little yoga; and I'm fucking cold.*

The cold had settled into my bones to stay and the transference and PTS symptoms were running amok again, yet all I managed to express to Trey was, "I want to go home, but I don't know where that is, and I don't know what it looks like."

The evening before our thirty-second anniversary, Trey, equally concerned and frustrated, booked my flight to Austin while I reserved a one-bedroom condo. Four days later he drove me to the Denver airport and I flew to Austin. Landing in the late evening, I texted Trey to advise him of my safe arrival while waiting for a rental car for the drive to the Clarksville neighborhood, where my next "home" was located.

I struggled finding the condo's correct parking space, pulling my luggage up three sets of stairs, and opening the key lockbox. Inside, the streetlights shone through the shades enough that I didn't need lights. Making my way to the bedroom, I dropped my luggage, fell into bed and slept solidly for the first time in weeks.

The sun was up when I awoke. Birds were singing, but they sounded different. Not different in song, just clearer, unmuddled, like when I was a young girl waking up on Westward Street.

For a fleeting moment, I remembered what that felt like, and what it felt like to be me.

• • •

The condo was walking distance to pretty much everything I needed, including a yoga studio, so I returned the rental car after retrieving my bicycle and yoga mat from storage. I contacted a few friends and, using the cold as an excuse, let them know of my early return.

Regular sleep and yoga gave me clarity, and the solitude provided enough freedom from moral conflict to consider what I needed to think about.

How do I move forward?

For much of the past three years, I had felt like one of those leaves in the wind vortex, and it had to stop. I was tired of the swirling, the dizziness, the storms, the searching, my feelings, and all the questions.

I can't run from this anymore.

PART SIX

NOT LIVING FROM A PLACE OF LOVE

Live with an open heart—be love,
live your truth, and trust that the
magical Universe is listening and
weaving away at you in a most
glorious and undefinable way,
for labels cannot yet exist for
you as you are a constant
evolution – a mystical
recipe – that can
only be known
at the end

Chapter 21
ON MY OWN

As a way to justify—and perhaps lay blame for—my inability to make my feelings for Dr. Kaye go away, I questioned everything in and about my marriage. I admitted my desire to please, remain a family, and subdue Lindsey's anger had driven my eagerness to salvage the marriage two years prior. I questioned if I had really wanted to enter into a relationship with Trey in the first place. I was only eighteen and worked with him and liked him, but he was married.

He'd look at me with a weird smile and gleam in his eye that scared me and seemed to steal a bit of my soul. He was assertive—he always knew what he wanted—and I was unsure and afraid. He also seemed somewhat desperate after ending his first marriage, one that had taken place when he was nineteen. *Had I been his rescuer?*

How far I had run from my eighteen-year-old self! I was a solar system away from that girl who had given Trey a chance, that neglected girl raised in a bio-dome where mere kids married and had babies because the murky atmosphere limited outlooks and thwarted prospects. I had never reckoned with that girl, and I wasn't reckoning with her now.

Although I loved Trey, I questioned whether I ever experienced romantic love with him, and whether I had really wanted to marry him. Did I marry by my own desire, or had I gone along because it was what he wanted? I was pregnant. Did I get pregnant because I wanted a family who loved and accepted me, and he offered such an opportunity?

Our daughters' births had induced within us a parental maturity along with an unbending determination to nurture them, meet their emotional and physical needs, and raise them into confident, thriving girls, teens, and young women. We took interest in their interests, supported their dreams and education, and they blossomed. As a family we flourished—four strong walls bound together in love openly expressed. But sometime between my mother's decline, her death and the reconstruction of my jaw, our daughters became independent women and had bought their own homes. During a time of disorder and instability, our four walls became two, revealing the delicate viability of their foundation.

While the marriage had been mostly fulfilling with thirty-two years comprised of great memories, enough not-so-great memories lingered to justify my wanting to end it. Subjects Trey and I had discussed two years earlier, but I had not yet made peace with. I don't know, maybe I had, and just needed to keep them alive in order to support my position.

Truth is, I simply didn't want to be married, and hadn't since I stood in that dark rainy field listening to Steve Winwood sing about higher love.

• • •

I wasn't sure of how to move forward or even what my new life might look like. Releasing the senses of uncertainty and future challenges on the yoga mat helped me maintain grounding, calm, and clarity of what I needed to do, but only from one day to the next. And that is all I needed. I now understood my Warrior II mantra – the gift of vision relates only to as far as I can see, which in that pose, is as far as the fingertips. A friend later told me of a Psalms verse that references a "lamp upon my feet." It's the same thing; the call is to follow your light, the inner voice that guides you, whether or not you know what is around the corner and regardless of social "norms" or perceptions thereof.

Since returning to Austin, I had longed to get out in nature and chose a warm morning in early February to rent a car and wend my way through the Texas Hill Country to Enchanted Rock State Natural Area. The trip's purpose wasn't to seek or receive guidance in nature on how to step out of my personal vortex. I just knew I needed to go.

After parking at the base of the "Little Rock," I grabbed my water bottle, and headed up its vast pink granite dome. For what seemed like the first time ever, I moved at my own pace and chose my own path. At the apex, I cut down and west toward the larger dome and a cluster of giant boulders with enough mass to keep them from sliding off the sloping face.

Inching down among the boulders, I sheltered myself from the view of other hikers. With Texas' wilderness rolled out before me, I sat down cross-legged, removed my boots, and closed my eyes. As the sun warmed my face, I felt the massive rock supporting my body. Concentrating on my breath, I acknowledged my pain and dilemma, filled myself with air, and released everything with an exhale. Sensing nothing but the immensities surrounding me, I found stillness and settled in silence within my internal world. Faint tints of green and purple hues danced behind my eyelids and grew more vibrant with each breath. Just as I had while meditating on the rooftop deck, I connected to the oneness of the Universe.

That is where the guidance comes from, and this is what that connection told me…

> "The head, the voice, and the heart are made to work in tandem. If one of them is not allowed to function as it's meant to, if it is suppressed, the others will surely suffer."

The message was clear and correct. I had not lived that way and it was hurting me. If I wanted out of the vortex, I had to sync my voice with my head and heart. I had no choice.

Truth. Is. Sacred.

I hiked eight miles that day, ending with an off-trail trek up the eastern face of the larger dome. Steep and challenging, I cut up it on a whim just to prove I could do it.

Fear can longer be my guide.

• • •

Since leaving Colorado, Trey and I communicated daily. I sent him an email following my epiphanies at Enchanted Rock, sharing my insight that, "I need to start loving myself enough to stop treating my needs and wants as expendable."

I told him I needed to grow back into myself and live authentically instead of trying not to disappoint the people I love, including him. Taking my email as a positive sign, he was ready to return to Austin. He perceived the words' meanings in a way that best fit into what he wanted, just as I had done during encounters with Dr. Kaye. Trey arrived at sunset on Valentine's Day. I met him in the parking lot to help him unload the Escape, and he greeted me with an ardent kiss.

As I recoiled, we both realized our understandings of the status of our relationship were misaligned. I re-read my email; parts were ambiguous. If I were to move forward, I had to work on being more direct and honest with Trey.

But Trey had already felt what was lacking in my kiss. More hard conversations—those of a certain level of honesty and intimacy—should have taken place. But that had never been our way because those types of conversations would have first required the vanquishing of Trey's defense mechanisms, and both my fear and desire to please.

I was still working on those, and Trey had always needed black and white; in not so quiet desperation he demanded it. "You love me or you don't; you want to be with me or you don't."

For me to accommodate that need once again was easier, except this time, it wasn't what he wanted. We agreed to divorce two days after his return.

I could not continue in the marriage as it was, which was not terrible by most measures, but it was not healthy for me. The storms would always return, and I was so ready to free myself from them. I was prepared to deal with my transference issue, and to align my heart, head, and voice along with all aspects of my being, all my various selves, and start living wholly. My truth, once again, was forcing me to do so.

Trey planned to travel to Europe while I found a place of my own in Austin and worked toward creating a life defined solely by me—I would pick my own pace and path. We remained in the little condo together and then moved to a tiny studio cottage in the same neighborhood where we sorted out the details of un-marrying. With cordial cooperation, we came to agreements on even division of our assets.

For two reasons, I delayed finding my own space longer than I should have. First, Trey expected us to live together until his April departure for Barcelona. Next, I was determined the process remain as copacetic as possible, even as the cottage walls seemed to close in on me.

The evenings together were suffocating since they demanded we ignore our waking-life reality while lying side-by-side, an arrangement Trey clung to and I enabled. *I'm again that person who contorts as necessary.*

Just as in our marriage, I accommodated Trey's needs, maintained façades to keep peace, and in doing so, ignored my reality. That hypocrisy was the true origin of my storms. Denial of truth, which I learned from my mother and the entire silent generation.

While driving to Houston, another aspect of my storms surfaced. The divorce had been my doing, so I wanted to inform family members. As I headed east out of Austin, a rage swelled up and out of me. I was angry about what I had to do. Without considering my own roles and mistakes, I was furious at Trey for everything he had done that led me to be in that car driving to Houston in the rain; I was incensed because he had not been what I wanted and needed him to be; and predominately, I was enraged that the whole thing had positioned me to fall in love with my doctor. The rage roared from me in the form of screams. I turned up the radio to drown myself out and then screamed for thirty miles. I screamed until I had no voice; and I screamed until my throat bled.

I thought I'd let go of my anger two years prior when our relationship changed, when Trey had opened himself to growth, and I decided to make the marriage work. But the past's scars still hung inside me, as I wrote in my journal, "like charred wallpaper flaking at the corners and revealing light from underneath. I have to work on peeling away the charred panels and then I will be fine. I have to do this alone."

After my return from Houston, I searched for my own place.

• • •

Despite my efforts to recognize when fear guided my actions, anxiety prevailed at times following the decision to divorce. Like when I contacted my old boss in an attempt to regain some semblance of my prior work life. My fear preferred going backwards into the known and comfortable, and at times it was a struggle to keep placing one foot in front of the other.

I told Grace it felt like I was walking across a crevasse on a worn narrow plank and sometimes it would have been easier to just jump off. I wasn't proud of that, but death seemed like the only alternative when I lacked the will and strength to lift myself from the vortex.

Yoga, support from family and friends, along with guidance from Grace, helped me to understand I had the wherewithal to add a handrail to the plank and find stability and balance enough to get to the other side; or at least to go as far as I could see and my fingertips could reach.

About a month before Trey was to cruise across the Atlantic, I moved into a two-bedroom duplex in north Austin. The rental was a blank slate, as was my life. I stood alone in the dining nook off the patio where I would begin writing this book and leaned onto a mountain of unpacked boxes to take a call from my former employer's HR Director, the same guy that I once believed had conspired with the FBI that fateful morning two and half years earlier. He offered me choices on jobs and asked me to name a salary.

Looking around my empty duplex, I told him I wanted to think about it. Despite my financial insecurity and my ego's yearnings, an immediate return to work was not what I needed. Instead, starting on the most simplistic of levels, I would give the decisions on how to recreate my life the time they deserved. I had to unpack my boxes and create a space in which I could live and breathe with ease; a space that reflected what was on my inside. I needed to work on myself – be alone with my truth and figure out what to do with it. I needed to deal with the holes the transference had filled, explore them carefully and with time.

Trey was supportive and filled his time with prepping for his travels. He had not once expressed bitterness or anger – he had been nothing but helpful. When I arranged to move into my own place before his scheduled departure, his feelings were hurt, yet he cooperated and even assisted with my move.

As I drove him to the airport, Trey released the weight of his suppressed reality. He wept and admitted that he had been hoping I would change my mind. I was taken aback but not unsympathetic. He was still crying as I pulled up to the terminal. I worried he would not make it through security unless he pulled himself together and tried to convey that as I hugged and kissed him goodbye.

He did make it through security, and eventually across all of Europe, just fine. Our divorce was finalized two weeks after his departure while he was on the Portuguese island of Funchal.

Chapter 22
THE SPACE TO BREAK

I embraced the solitude of my new home. I had much to contemplate, much breathing and processing to do; processing that I, alone, had not allowed. It took me a while to figure that out.

Grace had counseled me during the initial divorce process, which was helpful. But now, I was ready to discover the next steps forward on my own. I was up to the task and ready to rely on my inner voice's guidance.

I created a workspace, wrote down notes of self-assurance as they came to me and placed them under my desk's glass top or around my computer monitor. Statements such as, "I will get there," "You have to do the work," "Hard like a diamond," and "This is what it looks like."

Soon I recognized what distinguished my needs from my wants and took inventory on what those were… *I need a good night's sleep, yoga, and creative outlets; I want to decorate my duplex and find a job.*

And I made to-do lists—daily, weekly, and monthly lists—for everything from unpacking to personal exploration and expansion. Not everything would be crossed off at the end of the day, week, or month, and that was okay. Some of the days' sole achievements were cooking a creative meal or watering plants.

The lists kept me moving. I made progress, and a path was forged.

• • •

One of my wants was to "Travel – hike & explore," and ten days after Trey took off for Europe, I borrowed his camping gear and headed to the

Wichita Mountains, which is where I had wanted to hike when I returned from Colorado. Instead, I had opted for Enchanted Rock due to its proximity to Austin and Trey's apprehension of my camping alone. I'd freed myself from Trey's fears and now had only my own to confront.

I wanted to climb Elk Mountain again. Last May, I had stumbled and broken my ankle. Now, I was ready to conquer it and prove to myself I could camp alone. The experience would be empowering and help me work on my brave. Brave, as a state of being, seemed theoretical, existing externally. Brave was the state of existence I strove to achieve because of what I had to do next. I wasn't sure what that was as I traversed through rattlesnake country, over rocks and into narrow grassy passages, on my way to the summit. Something was there, though, just beyond my fingertips.

On the drive home, clarity came with the open road and sky, *I have to tell him.*

It was time to contact Dr. Kaye and have the conversation that should have taken place three years ago. And I would need to do it soon. I gave myself a week.

Over the course of that week I realized that clearing myself from the vortex required processing all the emotions that accompany falling in love with an impossible someone. My mind, and later my voice, already accepted that I had fallen in love with my doctor, but another level of acceptance awaited. I had to accept it through my actions; I had to own it. I would have to quit protecting myself and allow my heart to break.

Love, like grief, is too powerful to control, it's *not* something you can simply slap an "acceptable label" on in order to restrain or disregard.

• • •

After returning from the camping trip, I awoke to find an odd creature secured to my bathroom wall above the towel rack. It looked like a cross between a fly, a mosquito, and a cricket. As I leaned in to take a closer look, the little guy's antennae shook in fright – a sign that the insect, or whatever it was, was harmless.

The following evening, I hosted a friend for dinner, assuring her the creature was innocent and had not moved since first appearing in my bathroom. We laughed at its oddity and apparent terror at having its space invaded.

"If it's still there tomorrow, I'm going to give it a name."

Three days later I arose with a clear sense of what I had to do that day – like I had no choice; so I picked the time of 4 p.m. to call and leave word for Dr. Kaye. As that time approached, I longed to have someone with me when I placed the call. I wouldn't get through to Dr. Kaye, but just placing the call and talking to the receptionist would be brutal.

I thought of Jack McFly who had clung to my bathroom wall for the prior four days. He was the only other living being in my house. *I'm not really alone.*

Sipping on chamomile tea, I took my phone into the bathroom, inhaled the scent of a fresh lavender leaf, and lit a candle, transforming my bathroom into a calming room. I entered Dr. Kaye's office number into my phone at 4:05 p.m. and froze. *I don't have to do this today.*

A sense of knowing overcame me as my internal voice said, *"Yes, you do."*

My niece had posted a meme on Facebook that I had identified with, Proverbs 31:25, "She is clothed in strength and dignity. She laughs without fear of the future."

I recited it again and again. *I can do this.*

At 4:30 p.m., I hit the green "send" icon and left a message for Dr. Kaye to call. Afterwards I was elated; I had taken another step forward, a necessary one.

I looked up to where my friend had perched in support to say thank you, and to thank the Universe. Jack McFly was not there. For the first time in five days he was crawling, inching along near the ceiling toward the bathroom door. I looked for him again after returning the space back into a bathroom, but he had disappeared.

By 6:30 p.m., I exhaled with relief... it was probably too late in the day to expect a return call. The next day my actions were less ridiculous. I practiced my script before rising and going about my day. My phone was redlining, so I plugged it in to charge and set it on an elevated windowsill in my bedroom with the thought that its ringer could be heard from that location. Turning toward the bathroom, I caught a glimpse of something black just behind the top of my dresser. When I leaned in for a closer look, Jack McFly took flight around my bedroom and came to rest on the window blind above my phone.

He can fly?

My duplex was coming together beautifully. I'd hung every frame myself, assembled shelves and a platform bedframe, designed and built a headboard, and arranged and rearranged furniture until satisfied each space reflected my true self.

I had yet to deal with the spare bedroom and its stacks of file boxes. The boxes held chaos and emotions—Trey's and my personal records from our thirty-two years together, and my parents' records covering their time in my care—so I had avoided them. That morning, I assigned myself the mission of disseminating the boxes' contents into either a file cabinet, a box labeled "Trey," or a shredder.

The job required focus, which kept my mind distracted from the other impending task set in motion with the previous day's phone call. I was balancing on hands and knees over stacks of paper spread across the floor when my phone rang. My heart pounded as I walked into my bedroom and picked up my phone.

Breathe. I can do this.

I gave a grateful nod to Jack McFly, thought of the Proverbs stanza, and then, "Hello, this is Martha."

After exchanging hellos, I went off script, "I wanted to talk to you… ah… to let you know that I'm writing a book about my transference issue… that I know you know about, in fact, you probably knew before I did."

"Yes. First priority, though, is your health. Is everything okay with your jaw?"

"Yes, I'm fine. But you can't be my doctor anymore." My voice quivered. "I'm sorry… this is very difficult for me."

"It's okay."

"I see my primary care physician next week and I'm going to ask her for a referral to another surgeon."

"I understand." He seemed to already have another physician in mind, describing his demeanor and personality to assure I would be comfortable with him.

"Thanks, I'll check him out, and I need to make sure he's in my insurance network."

"Sure. But again, I think you'd really like this guy. He… um, he'd keep everything confidential."

I told him I would consider it, but after hanging up I was somewhat mortified. *This "gregarious guy" knows some silly female OMS case fell in love with his colleague and, as a favor, agreed to take on the poor soul—me!—as a patient!*

Above all else, I was proud of myself. It was another step forward, as I wrote in my journal, "I just need progress to somewhere."

The pain came later that afternoon. Somehow, not having that conversation allowed me to keep my feelings, and the overall experience, within a protected realm where I could doubt, question, and bargain. And, regardless of how poorly I had handled it, the phone call acknowledged my truth and exposed my heart to Dr. Kaye and the subsequent pain. I hadn't realized just how much pain. The floodgates holding back my emotions were released and forced me to swim with my pain. Over the following weeks it came in waves and knocked me to the floor.

Massive, unrelenting rogue waves assailed me for hours as I lay crumpled on the floor, blinded by the force of my tears. I could feel the hurt deep inside me swelling up from a seemingly endless well, and I surrendered to it.

Not just the wrenching pain of a broken heart was released; I was fractured by the fact that the transference had occurred in the first place, and horrified at the recognition of my own vulnerability. Then there was the sorrow and deep sense of loss for my mother whose presence I could still feel. I grieved for her and dad; they had never really known me. I mourned for all our conversations that never took place, and the relationships we didn't have because vulnerability and truth were such insurmountable obstacles.

I preferred to be alone with my heartaches. During walks around Lady Bird Lake, I stopped at the water's edge when the emotions intensified, and I let my tears flow. I hiked the same greenbelt trail where I first romanticized about Dr. Kaye while trying to keep up with Trey's pace, except I stayed present and allowed the trail's beauty to pacify my heart.

I tried rereading Carl Jung's, *The Psychology of the Transference*. During my first attempt, the text was too meaty and its alchemy references a bit farfetched. But the second time, after I had spoken to Dr. Kaye, words such as "rapport" and "connection" had me collapsing to the floor again.

Yet, unlike the challenge of crossing the crevasse toward divorce and an unknown life, my anguish never felt impossible. I respected my pain and allowed it to surge from me. And progress, albeit nonlinear, was apparent. Through May and June I endured, and ultimately arose from crying that I had not deserved the transference, to standing and accepting that perhaps I had.

The transference had compelled huge changes in my life, changes that probably would not have taken place otherwise. It pressed me to embrace my truth and use my voice, and it forced both Trey and me to open and grow.

Chapter 23
WITHOUT ILLNESS

Through the years of trying to deny, rationalize, and let go of my feelings for Dr. Kaye, I had only succeeded at letting go of everything else... my home, most of my possessions, my job, and my marriage. My initial recognition of this knocked back to the floor. But through the processes of exploring my holes and allowing pain, I gained healthier perspectives and discovered something completely unexpected—compassion for myself.

Yes, what I had been through had been hard. Much of the disorder I had navigated over the last three years was not of my own making, and what I had created was born from those self-preservation skills—the behavior systems and coping mechanisms I had developed as a child. Considering everything I'd been through, I had done my best. I had survived. *I truly am a strong and powerful warrior.*

Now I was working toward creating a new life, one based on who I am, my sacred truth... a truth not founded on fears, perceptions, or perceived standards of an abstract society, or any other construct. *Maybe the transference had been a gift, my struggles a blessing.*

Once I owned my feelings for Dr. Kaye and consciously acted upon them, I was, at last, in a position to progress beyond them. My heart had been properly broken, and I was tired of carrying the weight of the entire experience.

The persistent searching was like a muscle memory in my brain, a reflex had been switched on and had gotten stuck. My desk abutted a large window and I had no problem focusing on tasks, but part of me noticed every car that passed and became particularly alert with slow moving cars.

Nowhere to the extent as during my hyper-vigilant states, when I irrationally searched for Dr. Kaye during work commutes or at football games. Not even close, but the deep need to search for him had not completely quieted, and I didn't know how to turn it off.

• • •

Since his departure, Trey and I kept in regular email contact, and he and our daughters connected weekly via a video app. He kept me apprised of his travel experiences, and I updated him on the rising levels of Central Texas lakes. The rain had started in mid-May and stopped only after devastating floods, which helped the lakes recover from the prior years' drought.

By June, Trey and I had our own face-to-face internet conversations. Just seven weeks had passed since we'd seen each other, but we had both changed. We had grown – a bittersweet realization acknowledged through tears on both sides.

We each confessed to experiencing bouts of loneliness, and I shared my itch to travel beyond the Wichita Mountains. Straightway, Trey proposed I meet him in Venice and accompany him to Croatia. It sounded nice, but his eagerness scared me. Although I missed his companionship, such a rendezvous would not be a good idea for either of us, so I searched for a different option.

Maybe Trey's enthusiasm influenced my quick resolution, or perhaps it was this vision – I noted it the evening after Trey's invitation...

> "A beautiful large cluster of orange blooms glowed brilliantly through branches and the dark green leaves that surrounded it. (I feel this is a sign that I will have someone to love. A recent worry of mine.)"

Costa Rica had been on my bucket list, and the idea to travel there had been planted weeks prior when I received a newsletter from an Austin yoga instructor. I no longer had the newsletter but found the instructor's email address and contacted her for information. From that point, everything fell into place.

She was hosting a yoga retreat on the Nicoya Peninsula the week of July 4th. The resort looked amazing and a few spaces were still available. The next day, the resort manager contacted me and confirmed my spot, after which I booked the cheap flights I had found and held the previous day.

• • •

Over the remainder of June and through my scheduled departure for Costa Rica, I kept loneliness at bay by fulfilling my desire for forward progress. I developed a strategic plan that included a personal mission statement with supporting strategies and tasks as pathways toward what I envisioned as a "fulfilled, purposeful, engaging life." In accordance with the plan, I drafted a résumé, constructed an online professional profile, and initiated networking meetings, all to find the perfect job.

I also enrolled in an adult learner's program at a local university, joined a women's communicators group, trained as an American Red Cross volunteer, began weekly dance classes, joined a writing meet-up group, started drawing again, established a practice plan for learning the violin, and began exploring yoga teacher training opportunities. No time remained for loneliness.

During this period, Trey came to realize that six months was more than he wanted to travel across Europe and cancelled his October cruise reservation, leaving his return open-ended. We talked often. I told him of my scars from the unhealthy aspects of our marriage. I shared that my next relationship would be by my choice and not from feeling pressured; it would include one-hundred percent respect for individual identity and space, regular and equal exchanges of positive energy, and mutual respect, support, and consideration for each person's feelings, wants, and needs.

Trey knew what had caused my scars and why they had surfaced. I was looking for a job on the same professional and salary levels that I enjoyed before. Levels in which I had more than enough brains, knowledge, and experience, but that also required college degrees.

Trey had refused to support my education needs and desires—a broken promise, and the greatest betrayal of my soul. To maintain peace and stability for my family, I had accommodated Trey's insecurities, financial and otherwise, because the alternatives always seemed to lack the security I needed. They were unknown, too hard, and scary.

Now truth forced me to let go of the need for security and advance into an unknown future. I had crossed that crevasse, and I had crossed it alone.

He apologized again. "Believe me, if there was anything I could go back and change, I would."

I could not change the past either. I accepted that, but hadn't yet come to peace with it. For decades Trey's words, "I don't want you to go to school because I'm afraid you'll get too smart and leave me," had echoed through my mind like a hollow stone.

I had yet to find compassion for Trey and his abandonment issues. Nor had I come to recognize the direct and enabling roles I had played in the construction of my own limitations. I would have to find acceptance of and forgiveness for myself before I could grant the same to Trey.

• • •

Costa Rica was my first solo international travel experience, and I was giddy as I arrived at the San Jose Santamaria Airport. It was bustling, and I was herded through baggage claim and customs before being thrust outside among zealous taxi drivers. Thanks to another American tourist, I found my way to the shuttle provided by the hotel where I had arranged to stay for the evening.

The next morning, I caught a puddle jumper across the Gulf of Nicoya to the Tampor Airport where a taxi would be waiting for me. The plane seated about ten people, and the pilots were very careful on the total weight. Not only was my luggage weighed, but I also had to step onto a scale while holding my carry-ons. *What a novel premise—assuring you never carry more than you can handle!*

I was thrilled at the adventure and remained mesmerized throughout the flight, even as wind gusts knocked around the plane and passengers. Never had I seen such luscious green mounds rolling up to form mountains, nor had I imagined water appearing as a palette of swirling greens, turquoises, and blues. I laughed with elation.

The Tampor Airport comprised no more than two rows of covered benches, a small wooden structure resembling a concession stand, and a landing strip carved out of the jungle on the ocean's edge. I grabbed my luggage, paid a $2.25 tax for something and, not seeing a taxi, sat down on a bench to wait.

Most of my fellow passengers were gone or heading away when I overheard someone say "Anamaya," the name of the yoga resort. The driver's English was about as good as my Spanish, but at least we connected.

Miguel had been there all along. My mistake was looking for a typical American taxi. *I'm not in Texas anymore.*

As Miguel handled the luggage, I climbed into his red Jeep Liberty, and we headed out of the airport's gravel parking lot. I had no idea which direction we traveled or even which direction we should travel. I hadn't consulted a map prior to the trip, which was completely against my nature. My nature up to that point anyway.

Even as a child, I needed to know exactly where I was at all times. My dad pacified this need by having me play navigator on trips to Oklahoma. I continued in that role throughout my life with Trey, including on our trek around the U.S. At first, we relied on a phone app, but I soon grew frustrated at not being able to see the smaller perspective of where we were alongside the larger perspective of where we were going. So, we ended up purchasing an old-fashioned reliable atlas somewhere along the east coast.

That day, after I climbed into the car of someone whom I trusted based on the warmth in his eyes and smile, I basked in my liberation from the ridiculous fears that once confined me. And I laughed at the notion of maps as we twisted through the jungle for forty minutes, slowing only to avoid potholes, other cars, and a large green iguana.

I knew exactly where I was; I was in myself. I was where I was, and that is all I needed to know.

Anamaya translates to "without illness;" essentially it means health. The resort sits above the beach town of Montezuma and provides a treetop vantage point of Costa Rica's Pacific coastline. If one were to travel there and do nothing but sit and observe, no time would be wasted, as the beauty alone is enough to gain healthier perspectives.

Along with twenty-five other females, and one male, of varying ages, backgrounds, and countries of origin, I made my way to Anamaya. All were also seeking empowerment and adventure.

Official introductions took place in an opening circle where we were asked what drew us to Anamaya and what we hoped to achieve. I was surprised by how many of the beautiful souls were battling self-image issues, but I was more impressed and inspired by their openness and honesty. Some were half my age, yet double my brave. Understanding and compassion were natural byproducts of the honesty, and all found comfort, camaraderie, and safety in the revelation that... *everybody struggles.*

In addition to yoga, the week's schedule allowed options for local activities. I surfed, swam, and floated in the warm Pacific without care for what I could not see. Outside of yoga, my favorite pastimes were reggae dancing in Montezuma and massages. I opted for an oriental head massage, thinking it would relieve some of the discomfort in the left side of my jaw and face.

The massage therapist detected the weight I carried. She also sensed the loss of my mother, a need for deeper healing, and when she worked the areas of my neck and throat, she told me to repeat her words, "I am okay to speak my truth."

After the session, I thanked her and shared my doctor dilemma and how painful the experience had been. She told me she had once fallen in love with her anesthesiologist and made special connections with clients many times. She left me with the contact information of a local woman she described as a healer and suggested I schedule an appointment before the week's end.

• • •

Karen worked out of her home, which she had named La Paz, or "The Peace" for this gringo. On my last full day in Costa Rica, I skipped morning yoga and met a taxi at the top of Anamaya's driveway. The trip was to take about thirty minutes.

This driver's English was slightly better than Miguel's. My Spanish had gotten worse, or rather I had lost confidence after offending a young woman and learning that Central Texas Spanglish doesn't always translate favorably in Costa Rica.

The route to La Paz was a narrow and rough dirt road that coiled through the jungle. Its potholes were larger and more numerous than the road from the airport, and we plunged through several muddy water crossings. I couldn't help but laugh at seeing the road as the perfect metaphor of itself. As the driver slowed to cross one of the water crossings, I motioned her to stop so I could take a photograph of the road to peace.

The driver pulled into La Paz, indicated she would wait for me, and then pointed to a wooden staircase attached to a small wooden house, separated from the main house by a common landing. I knocked on the door at the top of the stairs and a small-framed, delicate woman with graying hair and a gentle smile greeted me.

She invited me in and handed me a clipboard with a release form. I took a seat on one of two padded dining chairs facing a massage table. The room was simply furnished and lit by the sun coming through a single wood-framed window that I had been facing, but didn't notice until after I returned the form to Karen. Clusters of orange hibiscus flowers jutted from a leafy branch about ten feet outside the window, just like my vision.

I'm where I need to be.

Karen sat down facing me and asked why I was there. I hadn't thought about what I would say. I just started rambling without a filter. My other selves were too tired, or maybe I trusted her. The road had shown me that getting to peace was treacherous, but I had been perfectly safe all along.

"I have a memory of my mother from the womb. I can feel her."

She gazed at me with sympathy. Not because she thought I was foolish, but because she understood that level of connection.

"I had some major surgeries around the time she died and then fell in love with the surgeon. When I was young, I had imaginary doctors instead of imaginary friends."

Her hands flew up, signaling that I need not say more, and she shook her head as her hands landed back on top of her thighs. Leaning in, she said, "Your inner child is misbehaving. When you ignore her... well, it's like a negative attention thing."

She told me to lie down on the table. "Let's introduce you to her."

She left the room while I moved to the table and got comfortable. She returned after a few minutes and placed a sleeping mask over my eyes. There may have been some guided breathing exercises to relax, but I don't remember, nor do I recall what she said to get my brain to enter the dream-type state.

I walked down a dirt road with my father. It was sunny and fields of

yellow wildflowers aligned both sides of the road. We approached the
ruin of a home and stopped at a stone opening leading to its basement.

I had dreamt this before, which is probably what invoked that particular
image. In the dream, my dad led me to the remnants of his mother's house.
All that was left was an opening in the ground and stone steps leading down
to a basement that I was too afraid to enter.

Karen's voice asked me where I was. I told her, and she told me to walk
down the stairs.

I left my dad and headed down the stone steps. There were a lot of steps,
they seemed not to end.

Karen's voice told me to keep going. She told me to tell her when I
arrived at the bottom.

"Okay."

"Where are you?"

"A grotto. It's beautiful."

"Good. Do you see anyone else?"

"No."

"There's a girl there. Do you see her?"

"Yes, now I do."

"What does she look like?"

It was hard to tell Karen. It wasn't a pretty sight.

I cried for the little girl. I felt bad for her, and I felt her shame. "She
has scraggly hair. There's dirt on her face. Her t-shirt is dirty."

Karen told me to clean her up and change her clothes.

I soaked a cloth in the grotto's water and started with her face, then arms and legs. I washed her hair and gently combed the tangles out and away from her face. I helped her into a new white dress and tied the sash behind her.

The little girl liked herself more. She seemed happy to be taken care of.

At Karen's directive, I knelt and faced her.

"I love you, and I promise I will always take care of you."

The girl was happy. Her joy swelled within me, took over my body, and burst outward in the form of laughter. She was laughing through my tears.

She was happy.

With my vision of the orange flowers, I'd hoped to find someone to love, I just hadn't expected that someone to be me. I promised to love and take care of the little girl inside of me and I felt her joy. She believed and trusted, probably a first for her.

In a journal entry that evening I wrote, "Heaviness gone." Walking through the San Juan Airport to depart Costa Rica, I stepped with a newfound lightness and consolidated focus.

Chapter 24
FILLING SPACE

The heaviness never returned, and the switch in my brain stuck in search mode was turned off. The rudimentary part of my brain wired only for survival had been pacified, yet that was not the end of my healing and growth.

Examining my holes with compassion revealed insights into the reasons for their existence and an opportunity for reconciliation. No, I could not change the past, but I realized that I possessed the power to change how it was affecting me.

It's not about defeating my psychology, it's about respecting it—recognizing its origins with empathy.

Childhood neglect had taught me to not trust or rely on those I love, and it caused me to create imaginary doctors and escape into fantasy worlds. Not only did I finally reckon with that little girl, I sympathized with her and forgave myself for life choices that I had long questioned.

Her holes had been formed when she was too young to understand that they didn't belong to her; her holes were merely the effects of someone else's projections.

No one can fix me – I was never really broken.

As a young mother I was determined to be one that was affectionate, attentive, and supporting, and as an adult I'd made it a personal challenge to care for my mother better than she had cared for me, but in many other aspects I was my mother's daughter.

Many of those little girl's keen self-preservation skills—suppressing her voice, seeking security, showing no vulnerability, plus her array of pretenses and defenses—were cyclical behaviors I'd learned from my parents, as they had learned from their parents, and so on. While other behaviors—fears, hiding truth, distrust, and disappearing into my imagination—I'd created to protect myself as a child.

All these "skills" kept me from living fully as an adult. They also kept me from sharing what was going on inside of me and seeking help when the PTS symptoms initiated. My entire life I'd never risked exposing my vulnerabilities, and I had never completely trusted the one person in this world who loved me explicitly and wholly... Trey.

After promising my mom I would do so, I hadn't known what living fully meant. I didn't think about it beyond her unrealized dream of being a foreign correspondent. Truth is, I had never allowed myself to have such lofty dreams, which is probably why I tried to do everything, once I realized I had options.

Being raised in an environment that taught me, subtly and not so subtly, that I was not special, had blinded me to the notion of options. It taught me that my wants and needs, including self-care, were expendable, and caused me to rely on external sources, including the people I loved, for justification of my worth and existence. That had me holding them up to unattainable standards, which was the hardest thing I saw in myself. And that was one thing I had to forgive myself for and, more difficult still, ask the ones I love for their forgiveness.

My childhood residues had also caused me to ignore the faint internal whispers telling me all along that I was special. They were from that part of my being I had accessed only enough to get by while being careful not to overstep perceived bounds and roles that someone else had established.

Before I could change, I also had to recognize how I had granted power to perceptions over truth. I had to start respecting my truth and accept and embrace myself by connecting to my own personal sources of power, love and energy and say, "Hey, this is who I am. This is my truth, it is sacred, and I'm going to honor it in every way."

And therein is the definition of living fully.

To live fully means conforming to nothing except your own heart, taking care of your body *and* your mind *and* soul, treating yourself as your own best friend, nurturing important relationships, and recognizing and appreciating those who love and support you. It's being one hundred percent honest with yourself and others, and always acting upon that truth – if you are not progressing from a place of truth, you are moving in the wrong direction.

When living fully, you're open to and grateful for what *is* and what comes your way rather than constantly striving for control; you are guided by love and truth, not stifled by fear. Living fully has you loving and expressing yourself – all your selves.

For me, that's my yogi-self, my dancing-self, my writing-self, my artist-self, my adventurer-self, my smart, sassy, fun, fierce independent, and sucks-at-math selves, and yes, my I-fell-in-love-with-my-doctor-self.

Before I grasped the true meaning of living fully, I ended up letting go of everything. My experience was dark and terrifying at times. But in the end, I released everything external while my inside was liberated from fears, doubts, and defenses until all that remained was the part of me, my sacred truth, that I had never embraced... and I opened to trusting it. From that place of trust and love, I filled the remaining spaces, external and internal, and I merged into being my full and whole self.

Thriving from the experience required developing new self-preservation skills that I work on every day. Skills such patience, compassion, gratitude, loving and caring for myself, and acting upon my connection to the *Higher Love* I always feel but cannot label, project, transfer, or explain.

• • •

I experienced many things I cannot explain, and don't feel a need to. There are large gaps in science's understanding of the brain, even larger gaps in knowledge of the cosmos, and most scientists, if they want to retain credibility, don't even acknowledge the mystic.

We humans like our perimeters. In an attempt to fathom what we do not understand, we categorize and label. Yet, by their very definitions, these perimeters, categories, and labels are limiting. They keep our worlds small, contained, and comprehensible.

Three months after my experience at Enchanted Rock, I read an article in a favored science magazine[4] on ten "flaws," or evolutionary inefficiencies, of the human body. Number eight was the "misrouted" recurrent laryngeal nerve that passes information from the brain to the muscles that enable use of the voice box.

According to the article, the flaw is that the brain-voice connection is not direct because the nerve gets tangled with fetal tissue that moves from the neck into the chest during development. The tissue then grows into blood vessels, freeing the nerve and making it find its way back up to the throat. Which it does, but only after looping around the heart's aorta.

So, yes, the nerve that connects the brain to the voice holds onto the heart at its handle. I read from another source that both the laryngeal and cardiac nerves branch from the larger parasympathetic vagus nerve. *Maybe the head, heart, and voice are meant to work in tandem.* I don't know. But, with everything I experienced, I'm now incapable of operating otherwise. My head, voice, and heart are aligned and none are suffering.

I encountered the man from the football game, the one that seemed to know what was going on inside of me, around eight months after the game. He rode a bicycle, approaching an intersection in front of my office as I crossed the street. He smiled, lifted a hand to his fedora, and tipped his

---

[4] Top 10 Design Flaws in the Human Body, From our knees to our eyeballs, our bodies are full of hack solutions. Chip Rowe, Nautilus Magazine, May 14, 2015

head as he circled the intersection and turned back the same direction he'd come from.

I returned the smile and continued on my way. I don't know if he recognized me, and I don't know if he, or any of the individuals I encountered while hyper-vigilant, were angels or anything else other than ordinary people who appeared out of place. That is why I noticed them; even so, each individual had helped me.

The strange encounters were what I needed. I needed to know that I was not alone. Just as I had not wanted to be alone while talking to Dr. Kaye. The mysterious Jack McFly was there and disappeared the next day. I never saw him again, but may have swept up his carcass from underneath my printer cabinet when I moved out of the duplex. I couldn't tell for sure.

Healing the inner child may be cliché, but it also worked for me. A loving connection with my true self was established and the remnant PTS symptoms disappeared, dispersing the vortex.

Irrespective of whether these experiences were coincidences or actions of a loving, mystical, magical Universe, they were all helpful, and that's magical enough for me.

During my time in the duplex, music did not disappear from my life. The lyrics and melodies that drew my attention were ones that supported my feelings and desires for Dr. Kaye, because that is what I sought. Through my greater desire to move forward, however, I recognized and accepted the roles I had played in constructing my life—Steve Winwood's words guided my decision to enter into a relationship with Trey when I was 18 years old because that is what I wanted the words to do. If not, I would have looked for a different song. The true power rested with me all along.

Although not consciously, I was responsible for planting and cultivating the seed of gratitude – also what I needed, and what Trey needed, too. He found the time and space for introspection, facing his own hard truths and childhood residues, on 20-mile hikes along the Italian and Spanish coastlines and on mountainous trails in Croatia and Montenegro. Traversing across Turkey and Bosnia-Herzegovina he learned self-reliance and gained confidence. While sipping cappuccinos on Paris sidewalks and exploring the ancient ruins of Greece, Trey reflected on his defensive behaviors. He recognized how they had been more hurtful than helpful, and how they'd really been an expression of his fears. So, he let them all go.

A great expanse lay between us, and that space and the freedom from the bounds of marriage, both those set in law and within our own perceptions, finally provided an environment where we felt it safe to begin those conversations that required a "certain level of honesty and intimacy." The deepest level, actually; where all your selves, your heart, and parts of your brain are in agreement and act as one when you speak.

I told Trey of the pain I experienced. I told him how I contacted Dr. Kaye to at last acknowledge my feelings and allow my heart to break. I told him of the hours I spent on the floor. I spoke through tears, and as tears welled in Trey's eyes, he responded with sympathy, "I'm so sorry Mart, I had no idea you were in such pain."

Of course he hadn't. I had never owned my feelings and, beyond initially telling Trey the reason for my breakdown, we certainly never discussed them. The front I'd presented justified a psychological base; which it was, but that didn't mean my love was not real.

Humans are sensory-based beings. We can only experience and sometimes our experiences are solely internal. Chaos and darkness ensued whenever I denied and battled what was inside of me. Whenever I acted upon it—my truth—the course of my life shifted in dramatic and positive ways. I grew and I changed, and I'm not sure it can get any more real than that.

• • •

The rules governing travel between European countries under the Schengen Agreement influenced Trey's return in mid-August more than the fact that he'd grown weary of traveling, hiking, and eating alone. As his return date neared, my apprehensions and stress levels rose.

I was not confident he would respect my space, nor was I confident I would be steadfast in respecting my own needs and wants. I was still trying to figure out what those were. I didn't want to be alone, but earning trust and learning how to trust takes time.

So we decided to be friends – a door I willingly opened based on Trey's compassionate reaction to my broken heart. He shared his travel photos and adventures with me, and we reminisced on our travels together and the majestic beauty of the world. I told him how random memories from our U.S. trip popped into my mind throughout his time in Europe and even after his return. The recollections were of little things I had not known existed as memories. Such as crossing a log lying over a creek in the Montana wilderness, stoking campfire flames in Yellowstone, and saguaros' silhouettes against an Arizona sunset. Not just images came to mind, I recalled the feel of each place and how I felt while making the memories. Happy.

Before, I had clung to the negative memories that supported my desire to end our marriage and what I needed to do – move forward. We talked about those memories, too. We were both far from the individuals we had once been. No longer kids, and no longer weighted down by our and other people's literal and metaphorical stuff, we found the space to forgive and rediscover each other. We also took proper time to nurture the positive aspects of our relationship... the fun and adventure, the music, the affectionate banter, and our love of nature, travel, food, and each other.

His compassion for my broken heart, the memories of our travels, and creating, and continually cultivating, an environment for honest and respectful dialogue opened me up to trusting—and later relying on—Trey as an unwavering source of support. I grew to trust I could be the same for him while not losing myself. He is now a best friend and partner who one hundred percent respects my individual identity, space, feelings, wants, and needs. And although I'd never truly been imperiled, he's still willing to cover my shark-side.

With no more impossible expectations of what the other should be, visions for what we wanted our new lives to look like took form, and we agreed to respect the differences. The magical Universe responded, and everything simply fell into place. Job offers came, but with time and comprehension of what living fully meant, I came to honor my creative-self and my truth's callings more than my ego's need for validation, "professional liberation," and a financial safety net.

Instead, I observe, I think, and I express my truth through writing, art, and other creative means. I practice yoga daily, seek adventure and beauty, and continue to work on my brave.

I dance. I love. I live.

Near the healing waters of Lady of Bird Lake, I finished this book in our new permanent home and from the same iron rod-and-glass-top desk I bought on Craigslist. The heart-shaped rock I found after my breakdown sits next to my computer and serves as a reminder of how far I have come.

The new foundation Trey and I established is solid; we have no more than what we need or love, and all closets and hidden spaces remain uncluttered.

Mine is not only a life I can live. It is a life I love.

• • •

I now know what I should have done when I first experienced feelings for Dr. Kaye. I should have told him, and I should have told Trey. When chaos is inevitable, it is better to let it commence rather than contain. We humans operate best as open systems[5]. We're are built to process emotions,

---

[5] The 2nd law of thermodynamics states that within closed systems chaos exists, and will continue to increase over time. As living organisms, humans are naturally open systems-

not bury them.

The transference was a big red flag telling me to take inventory of and action on all the aspects in my life from which I needed rescuing. It was also a calling to both Trey and me to grow and change. Of course we didn't recognize that at the time, and if we had, I'm not sure we would have landed where we now find ourselves. And I'm not sure I would have come to release, respect, and love my voice and all my selves.

Yes, our individual, challenging, and wandering paths were necessary.

Climbing out of a comfortable rut is a tough ascent. It takes time and growth. It requires hard and scary, defeating insecurities, taking pain by the hand in order to let it go, and becoming aware of and correcting codependent behaviors, even when codependency is all you ever knew.

Yet it is a worthy endeavor, and I am most grateful that through my journey I endured, grew, and came to understand and begin living the deepest definition of living fully.

The Beginning

---

we dissipate energy while also receiving it from outside sources. When it comes to emotions, our rational and subconscious brains can hinder this exchange creating disorder.

EPILOGUE

Why I don't use the D-word...

The word disorder, in relation to post-traumatic stress, has a connotation of permanence. Such thinking lends itself to stigmatizing the condition as something uncontrollable, something to be ashamed of as if the symptoms were unnatural to the human experience. I refuse to support ridiculous stigmas by branding stress, that occurs naturally after a trauma, as a disorder.

In addition, the placement of "disorder" alongside "post-traumatic stress" completely disregards the initial disorder that created the traumatizing experience. The label ignores the truth that extreme chaos lacks control, safety, and predictability, and ignites the human brain's *natural* stress responders. Yes, the disorder first exists in the circumstances that cause our brains to react and process exactly as they should in order to gain an understanding of the chaos, and to contain and control it.

There are specific parts of our brain that help us to identify, understand and process perceived dangers, and I say "perceived dangers" because we are all different – the definition of dangerous is relative, it is unique to the individual. A simplistic explanation of the highly complex system that science doesn't fully understand is: our brains respond to stress through layered processes involving the amygdala (the fundamental survival instincts of fight, flight or freeze), the hippocampus (which is more reasonable and helps to temper the reactive amygdala), and the prefrontal cortex, the thinking, reasoning part of our brain that helps us rationalize.

And therein lies the problem... *How do you rationalize the irrational? How do you make sense of the incomprehensible? How do you assign order to disorder?*

You can't, but our brains are persistent.

I don't use the D-word because words matter, and I think it is most important for those suffering from post-traumatic stress to not be stigmatized with a label. It is paramount for them, and their loved ones, to understand that the brain can heal, just like the body can heal from other stress injuries. There are no stigmas attached to other strains; no one shies away from discussing a running injury, tennis elbow, or carpel tunnel syndrome!

We go to regular check-ups for our eyes, teeth, and reproductive and general health, while the brain—the control center for everything we humans do and experience—is our most important body part. Yet we fail to treat it as such; mental health doesn't become a concern until mental unhealth exists. Our society, and health care and coverage entities, fail at promoting the brain as an organ that should be cared for with the upmost respect. This confounds me. Why aren't brain wellness and preventative programs integral parts of our health care system, like mammograms?

If you've read this book, you know that my brain stopped functioning effectively and rationally, and that healing it was a challenging three-year journey plagued with setbacks. And hopefully you recognized that most of those setbacks were the result of my lack of will and self-care.

Through my story, it's also evident that my inability to ask for help, and accept or speak my truth, intensified the PTS symptoms compounding my illness. By sharing my hard truths, I am hopeful to normalize post-traumatic stress, reframe it as a difficult yet positive growth experience, and inspire others to avoid my mistakes.

I implore all those stressing over buried truths and traumas to seek assistance, it exists…

none of us are alone.

ABOUT THE AUTHOR

MARTHA J. MARTIN

Ms. Martin is a woman with an extraordinary story, relayed in her memoir *The Unintended Consequences of NOT Living Fully*.

Her writing and communications skills were honed over a twenty-six year career in state government, where she worked in the pension benefits sector and for the late Bob Bullock, in both his offices as State Comptroller and Lieutenant Governor.

She writes, meditates and practices yoga daily, dances often, and travels when she can.

She lives in Austin, Texas.

wewillfigureitoutblog.com

Author photo by Sara Jordan Photography

www.ingramcontent.com/pod-product-compliance
Lightning Source LLC
Chambersburg PA
CBHW071524040426
42452CB00008B/879